PAUL HEGARTY
Heading for Glory

PAUL HEGARTY
Heading for Glory

Foreword by
JIM McLEAN

JOHN DONALD PUBLISHERS LTD
EDINBURGH

John Donald Publishers Ltd.,
138 St Stephen Street, Edinburgh,
EH3 5AA.

ISBN 0 85976 206 8

My thanks to George Ashton and
D.C. Thomson Ltd. for permission to
use the photographs printed here and
to Kevin McCarra for preparing the
index.

Phototypeset by
Newtext Composition Ltd., Glasgow.
Printed in Great Britain by
Bell & Bain Ltd., Glasgow.

Foreword

Over the last ten years, when we have had reasonable success as a club, the unit this success has been built round was most certainly goalkeeper Hamish McAlpine, now with Raith Rovers, and central defenders Paul Hegarty and Dave Narey.

There have been others and there are others, but the base was laid by these three truly outstanding performers.

Paul Hegarty came to us as a striker from Hamilton Accies – and a good one. But one of his first experiences as a United player was sitting in a dug-out watching Andy Gray score a hat-trick against Partick Thistle.

Andy was one of the great strikers of his era and Paul was immediately made aware of the tremendous difference between the level of football he had been playing and the standard required of him now.

It could have shattered him completely, but he didn't give in.

The real turn-round, though, came with a change of position.

We decided to play him centre-half in a friendly against Everton, in direct opposition to Bob Latchford, a first-class striker winning England honours at the time.

He did an excellent job and hasn't looked back since.

He is a real credit to the club both on and off the field, an excellent ambassador.

We have had offers for many players. He was involved in one of the first big transfers we turned down, when Tottenham Hotspur wanted to buy him.

He accepted the directors' decision and has since given tremendous service to Dundee United.

Jim McLean
Manager, Dundee United F.C.

Contents

page

Contents

Introduction

My dream from the very first time I can remember kicking a football was to achieve top-class professional status in the game.

I believe I have succeeded in this by playing for Dundee United and Scotland and I have written this book partly as a 'thank you' to the many who have helped me achieve my ambitions to date and as a record of a career which has had its ups and its downs, but which has fulfilled the hopes of a young Edinburgh boy certainly up to and in some ways beyond his wildest expectations, with hopefully more to come.

The major achievements have come some 60 miles up the east coast of Scotland from my boyhood home, with Dundee United, a club which has, in my time, won its first major honours – league championship and twice the League Cup – and seen the first players ever at Tannadice, including myself, win international honours.

The architect of those triumphs – and they are major triumphs when set against the background of a provincial club – has been manager-coach-director Jim McLean. From being just another club, United are now ranked among the best in Europe as well as a major force in Scotland, largely because of the planning and application of this man.

So it is to him in my professional life that I say my first 'thank you.'

But being involved in the game at such a level is also down to your team-mates, and I have been privileged to play with so many outstanding professionals that I cannot possibly name them all.

If I single out my partner in central defence, Dave Narey, and the man who played behind both of us for so long and who gave so much entertainment, Hamish McAlpine, I do so only to illustrate the quality of those I have played alongside.

I could fill a chapter on its own simply by adding Frank Kopel, George Fleming, Alex Rennie, Paul Sturrock, Eamonn Bannon, Davie Dodds, Ralph Milne, Richard Gough, Ian Redford, Iain Ferguson, the up-and-coming Kevin Gallacher, the unsung but vital men in any team such as Billy Kirkwood and John Holt and so on and on. So I will abbreviate and to all I have played alongside say 'thank you' because it is a team game and achievement may come individually on occasions but mostly stems from being involved in a quality team, which Dundee United certainly have been in my time.

There is another side to life, of course. Off the field. And here again I could not have had better support and understanding than from my wife Linda, and from her family and mine. At times football can be all-consuming, and the man at the centre of attention must have support from those closest to him, even more so, understanding. I have had both in full measure.

The 'thank you's' go on and on and when you begin to think them over you realise you will inevitably miss out on some – for which I here and now apologise.

High up the list comes Andy Dickson, United physio for so long and now happily back with us – and his successors Bill Ramsey and Jim Joyce – for repairing the many bumps and bruises, and worse, that a footballer collects in his career; the directors of the club who have played a major part in its growth; friends in all walks of life, United followers and people who don't even follow the game never mind the club; and Ian Wheeler and Peter Rundo who have 'coached' me in the writing of this book and provided facts and figures.

And maybe, when it all comes down to the bottom line, I write for my sons Paul, Mark and Christopher as much as for anyone. I am proud of being a professional footballer, I am part of a great game worldwide, and I hope that they will in time read this and feel I didn't make a bad job at all of the only career I ever wanted.

1

Roller Coaster Season

On the evening of May 6, 1987, in Gothenburg, Dundee United were poised on the edge of one of the greatest club achievements of all time – a European and domestic Cup double.

In the late evening of May 20, 1987, only fourteen days later, the club was in deep, deep despair, two finals lost, everyone drained mentally and physically.

It was a shattering experience which will live with me and everyone connected with the club all our lives.

But, in my particular case, it was a mirror image of a roller coaster of a season, a season where events dipped and rose suddenly and violently throughout, where it was a case of heading for glory one minute and plumbing the depths the next.

The upward surge started early.

We had lost Richard Gough to Spurs after a few games, assistant manager Wattie Smith had gone to Rangers to join new player-manager Graeme Souness – and didn't they prove themselves in that amazing revival of the Ibrox club which saw them end by winning the League Cup and league championship?

With Davie Dodds and Hamish McAlpine, two outstanding players in their time with us, also no longer at the club, the prophets of doom weren't long in working out that we were in for a tough season.

They were soon having to make a considerable re-assessment as we moved steadily ahead in the league and League Cup and opened our account in Europe.

A great boost was our first league result against Rangers. We had three points from two games and were playing well when we visited Ibrox in the third game of the season.

They went ahead playing good controlled football, and it was understandable up to halfway through that the Ibrox legions on the terracing and in the stands were looking on us as cannon fodder.

But we came raging back second half and quietened them by winning 3-2, through two Kevin Gallacher goals and one from ex-Ranger Ian Redford.

Yet it was Rangers who also gave us our first real knock back of the season.

We had beaten Queen of the South, Ayr United and Hibs 1-0, 3-0 and 2-0 all away from home in the Skol League Cup and met Rangers in the semi-final at Hampden on September 24, just over five weeks after the Ibrox league victory.

I don't believe in hoodoo grounds or teams, but let's just say we again didn't do ourselves justice at Hampden and again lost out in a vital game against Rangers.

They beat us 2-1, their scorers Ally McCoist and Ted McMinn, ours Iain Ferguson, another former Ibrox man, who had joined us from there in the close season.

At this point he had played only seven games, but already had nine goals. That's what I call deadly finishing – and as an ex-striker and a long-time centre-half, I should know.

We had lost 1-0 away to French club Lens in the first-round first leg of the UEFA Cup, but that didn't worry us too much and we picked ourselves up from that and the disappointment of the Skol Cup result to beat them 2-0 at Tannadice.

On the night our scorers were Ralph Milne and Tommy Coyne – and at that time we didn't know that neither was to finish the season with us.

Tommy went 'up the road' to Dens Park, where he did well as a scorer in the remainder of the season and Ralph headed off down to England and Charlton Athletic. Ralph had been with us a long time, had scored some wonderful goals.

So now we were into October; the roller coaster had dipped with the Cup defeat, but risen because we were still in Europe and had no fewer than 19 points from 22 in the league.

As yours truly had also tucked away three goals, things weren't going at all badly.

Which brings us to October 11 and a visit to Pittodrie. They call Aberdeen and Dundee United the 'New Firm' because both of us had upset the dominance of the 'Old Firm' of Rangers and Celtic so often in the previous decade or so.

With the two cities being not too far apart and both teams doing well, there is always a great atmosphere when we play up there.

It was there again and I was raring to go as always, little knowing that this game was to be the start of a huge dip by the roller coaster as far as I was concerned.

I was up against former team-mate Davie Dodds most of the brief time I was on the park, and about the 20th minute we both went up for a ball. We bumped against one another in the air and I came down awkwardly.

I don't know if you have noticed, but most serious injuries happen without anyone but the player it has happened to being aware of it.

Our physiotherapist, Jim Joyce, came on and gave me treatment and I got to my feet.

When the game re-started, I lasted about two minutes. The pain was frightening and I couldn't get going. I signalled to the bench that I would have to go off. As I hobbled to the dressing room, Ian Redford took my place.

By a strange coincidence, Aberdeen centre-half Alex McLeish came walking down the tunnel just after me nursing a shoulder injury.

Someone who wasn't at the game could read into that that things were really physical on the pitch.

Nothing could be further from the truth. No one ever held back in games between the two clubs, but these two injuries were pure accidents.

I had landed awkwardly, Alex had been having shoulder trouble anyway and had aggravated it.

When my injury was finally diagnosed it was a severe strain high up in the left groin. For three or four days I did absolutely nothing but rest – I had no option!

Football is a team game. There is nothing a player likes better than training with his mates, playing, and taking part in the dressing room chat.

When you are seriously injured all that goes out the window. You are on your own and, no matter how you are treated, you feel right out of things.

As I gradually moved on to light exercises and eventually to working with the ball again, Dr Harry Leadbitter, the club physician, and physios Jim Joyce and Andy Dickson kept telling me 'Be patient . . . it'll take time.'

Even though a player knows this, it doesn't help. I doubt if any of us are good watchers of the game. I went to all the home fixtures, 'kicked' every ball and left with only one thing in mind – to get playing again.

And I did, 54 long, wearisome days later against Motherwell. It was December 3 and during my absence the league challenge had been maintained and we had won through two more rounds of the UEFA

Cup, 3-1 on aggregate against Universita Craiova and 2-0 on aggregate against Hajduk Split.

I felt great. I was back in the team and, as a bonus, we went 2-0 up in no time through Ian Redford and Jimmy Page. It was a night game on a heavy pitch and I was in my element . . . until almost exactly the same minute as trouble hit me against Aberdeen.

This time the other groin 'went', suddenly and without warning. What would the odds be against coincidence like that: similar injury, same time in the game? Heavy . . . very heavy.

There is a theory that I must have been 'favouring' the previous injury and put too much strain on the other side. I don't know about that, but I do know it was back to square one with the loneliness, the frustration of watching, not playing, and all the rest.

Funnily enough, just as Alex McLeish had come off right after me at Aberdeen, Maurice Malpas came into our dressing room at Fir Park before I had even sat down.

My immediate reaction was that he had been sent off, because he had shown no sign of injury, but it was a leg knock and he was to be out for a couple of games. Dave Beaumont took my place, Kevin Gallacher went on for Maurice.

This time I was out of action at first-team level for three months and one week – but not all because of that second groin strain.

The club arranged a game against Scotland's Under-17's at Tannadice and I was there, ready to come back into the first-team reckoning.

I was feeling great, moving freely when one of the young lads tried to chip the ball over our defence.

I'll swear I didn't have to jump more than six inches off the ground to get my head to the ball and clear it. I came back down perfectly, too.

But an instant after I hit the ground, a pain equal to that which hit me when the groin troubles started lanced up the back of my leg from achilles tendon to calf muscle.

This time it was in the second half of the game. I had to come straight off the park with my achilles severely damaged.

Talk about sickeners. I had been lucky with injury all my career. Even the cartilage problem against Norway hadn't kept me out that long and another cartilage injury had happened with the close season giving me plenty of time for recovery.

But here I was being hit by THREE injuries in different parts of the body, one after another and NONE involving a 50-50 challenge, or a

60-40 one for that matter, none involving any rough stuff.

It was that roller coaster on another of its downswings and it had me trying to remember how many ladders I'd walked under or mirrors I had broken!

So it was back to the treatment table yet again, back to the loneliness of the much-injured footballer, back to watching instead of being involved.

Not that the results were causing anyone connected with the club any heartaches. Apart from losing 2-0 to Rangers at Ibrox in the league, the challenge mounted from the first day had been kept up with a run of eight wins and three draws.

In the Scottish Cup the lads had a real tough one in Airdrie in the third round. They set about us like tigers at Tannadice and got a 1-1 draw, which they deserved.

They had high hopes of winning the return, but the old saying about never giving good teams a second go at you held good and, at Broomfield, the lads won through 2-1 with goals from Ferguson and Gallacher.

There was a trip to Brechin in round four and, though it maybe wasn't one of our most memorable performances, the result was right for us – a 1-0 victory via a Kevin Gallacher goal.

And all the time I was getting nearer fitness again.

The United roller coaster was on a 'high', mine on an upswing . . . and the best – and worst – was yet to come!

2

Two Finals

The season had boiled up for United. It was March, the league challenge was being maintained, the club was three games off the Scottish Cup final, six off the UEFA Cup final, and Paul Hegarty was – at last – really fit again.

I edged back into the reckoning for the first game against the Spanish giants Barcelona in the European trophy. I was on the bench and would have loved to have gone on, but it wasn't to be.

That said, I thought the team played great stuff and also must pay tribute to Barcelona for always putting skill first.

We got a 'flier' of a start when Kevin Gallacher sent in a looping cross from the right which completely deceived the Spanish defence, especially 'keeper Zubizarreta, and dropped into the net at the far post.

Terry Venables, the Barcelona manager, was later to call it a fluke, but they all count – and Kevin isn't slow to claim he meant the ball to go where it did.

Following his goal against Brechin, then this one against the Spaniards, Kevin had put us into the quarter final of the Scottish Cup and in a very strong position in the UEFA competition.

It was a marvellous night for the club and for the support who revelled in the game and the skills on show and were behind the team from first minute to last – even when, second half, Barcelona kept probing and trying to find a weakness and lots of hearts must have been in lots of mouths!

I couldn't believe it when the final whistle blew. It hadn't seemed like 90 minutes had been played, but they had and we all felt optimistic about the trip to Spain, even though I suspect Barcelona felt they now had the edge, being only one goal down and with the home leg to come.

My real comeback started ten days after the Barcelona game – in one which didn't quite have the same drawing power, but which was no less important!

It was against Forfar Athletic in the Scottish Cup quarter final. They aren't rated a big club, but over the years I have developed a tremendous respect for them under a succession of excellent managers. They play good football and are never easy to beat.

They certainly gave us a fright – a 2-2 draw at Tannadice before we put them out 2-0 two weeks later. Iain Ferguson, not surprisingly, scored in both games, but it was the other scorers who caused the raised eyebrows.

Maurice Malpas first game, John Holt second. Their only goals of the season – but they picked a great time to score them.

My first game in the league on my return was against Rangers, and they took the edge off our championship challenge with a 1-0 win at Tannadice.

The scorer was another striker who was having, like Iain Ferguson, a great season – Ally McCoist. A free kick was headed back across goal by Terry Butcher and McCoist tapped it in. The decision was given that he was not offside, but many United fans have since told me they are convinced he was.

Be that as it may, we lost the points and when we managed only three from the next four games we were down to challenging for the two Cups. Mind you – two out of three isn't bad, not bad at all!

Three days before this we had been in Barcelona and we had qualified for the semi-final of the UEFA Cup with a wonderful performance, which I will go into more thoroughly later in the book, rounded off perfectly by great goals from John Clark and Ferguson. An aggregate 3-1 against a team like that is great going – and if I have one slight disappointment it is that the 120,000 stadium wasn't packed rather than only one-third full.

There was a marvellous turn out by the United supporters and it was a genuine delight to all of us that we gave them so much to be happy about.

Now, the season really had taken off. We drew Borussia Munchengladbach in the semi-final of the UEFA Cup and our greatest rivals, Dundee, in the semi-final of the Scottish Cup.

You could feel the excitement everywhere on Tayside and the media pressure was also building up.

In the early stages of our European campaign we had three journalists covering our games, sometimes four or five.

When we got to Barcelona, the media 'corps' numbered about 50 – and if you take into account technicians it was probably nearer 100 by the time we reached the final.

Our coach Gordon Wallace joked that in the early stages, the media had only enough to make up one team for Trivial Pursuit, whereas, by the end, they could have fielded several full teams for football.

Mind you, in this amazing season we didn't only reach two finals, we were also the only British club in the later stages of the various European tournaments, so I suppose that made us unique and a natural for mass coverage. I know I have never spoken to so many reporters and into so many microphones.

Considering I was only about one-hundredth as involved on that side as manager Jim McLean, I don't know how he coped – but he most certainly did.

The roller coaster for both Dundee United AND Paul Hegarty was on a high, and moving higher.

Team changes were being made as the manager strove to keep us fresh. We played no fewer than 22 games in the final 77 days, or 11 weeks, of the season, including four quarter-final ties, three semi-finals and three Cup finals! We also travelled to Spain, Germany and Sweden in this spell.

It isn't easy getting it right in these circumstances when you have only a limited number of players and have to take injuries into account.

I have mentioned the Borussia games elsewhere. The biggest domestic event was the Scottish Cup semi-final against Dundee.

It was played at Tynecastle, which annoyed most of the support of both clubs. Despite their loud protests, though, it went on there and not at one of the 'home' grounds.

And I here and now claim it as one of the most exciting and crowd-pleasing games I have ever been involved in. Under manager Jocky Scott, Dundee have steadily improved and here they really set about us.

Usually in a semi-final everyone is tense and anxious and play suffers. Not this time. Most of the first half belonged to them. They went in 2-1 up and deserved it.

But our experience stood us in good stead. We didn't panic, kept playing to our strengths and pushed down the wide positions a bit more.

Before long we were in charge and it was the marvellous United following who were singing and chanting. Fergie brought us level, then my personal roller coaster, which had dipped so frequently in the season, soared to a new high.

Paul Sturrock crossed from the right and I got what turned out to be the winner. As the ball came over, Ian Redford and I went for it and I practically pushed him out of the way to score from my favourite distance – but not offside! – of half-a-yard.

They weren't finished by any means and came back at us strongly near the end.

Big John Brown, who has a marvellous shot from dead ball situations, let go with two of his very best from just outside the box, and to say that Billy Thomson made world-class saves as the ball dipped and swerved isn't to do him full justice. I still can't fathom how he got to the ball – twice.

When we added to this victory, beating Borussia in the second leg of the UEFA Cup semi 11 days later we were now in two finals – and, though we didn't know it then, were facing the most shattering experiences of our football lives.

First up was the UEFA final (first leg) in Gothenburg. That is without doubt a beautiful city and we were in one of the finest hotels it has ever been my privilege to stay in.

But I would have settled for a lot less of that and a lot better pitch in the Ullevi Stadium. A rock concert had been held on the pitch a week earlier and I wasn't prepared to argue that the playing surface had sunk several inches because of the weight of people and equipment on it.

The grass was loose, there were patches of sand. It was a disgrace of a pitch to play a final on.

It didn't help our cause any that Billy Thomson suffered a horrific ear injury early on and did tremendously well to carry on with blood and bandages all over the place.

Would he have got to their goal if he had been fully fit? I believe he would, even though Pettersson did well to get above the ball and head it down. What amazed me was the bounce the ball took. It ended up in the roof of the net when I'd have expected it to reach about half that height. Did it hit a hard patch on that disgrace of a pitch? Could be.

My injury worries were behind me, I was enjoying the game and didn't feel we had done badly or that we wouldn't be able to see things through successfully at Tannadice.

Then, second half, the ball was pushed past me towards the bye-line. I stretched for it – and over-stretched. I felt my hamstring go and even though I tried for another couple of minutes, I had to go off with John Clark taking my place. Another down . . . and worse and worse again was to follow.

Ten days later it was the Scottish Cup final against St Mirren and, at a personal level, the 'down' started early when I was left out of the team and named as a substitute.

We were favourites, hot favourites because of our marvellous Cup runs and the fact we had beaten St Mirren three times out of four in the league. And I wonder if that was part of our problem? We were far more used to being the underdogs. This time all the pressure was on us – and it showed.

If we had got going I believe we would have scored two or three goals, but we were edgey, didn't play anything like our best and they grew in confidence the further the game went.

Not that I didn't believe we would win – even into extra time I thought we could do it. But as both teams were showing signs that the humid atmosphere was sapping their energies, we were hit a tremendous blow.

The ball was pumped through to their Ian Ferguson and he did really well to keep going and hit it perfectly into the net behind Billy Thomson. They were on a tremendous high, we were devastated. Oh we tried to claw back into things – I know the effort that was put in because by now I was on in place of Ian Redford – but we failed.

All over the place our players sank to the ground and, later on, the dressing room was like a morgue. It was a long, long 85 miles back to Dundee in the team bus – especially as we kept passing cars full of United fans.

Some of them waved and shouted, but mostly they were just sitting there, like us, stunned.

There are those who say it was asking too much of us to then have to play the second leg of the European tie only four days later.

I don't see it that way. When we were beaten in the Scottish Cup final by Celtic we had a whole close season to brood over defeat.

Here, we had another Cup final to follow our defeat – and what is better at 'lifting' you than playing in a Cup final after a Cup final?

Again I had a personal disappointment in that I was again on the bench as a substitute, but I did get on, in place of John Holt, and I say here and now that everyone present will be proud to say ten, 20, 30 and more years from now, 'I was there', or 'I played in that final.'

Yes, we lost and I will never forget the scenes at the final whistle when, yet again, our players had to face the fact that we had failed. The pain was in their eyes, in their tears, in their drawn faces. But I believe we were entitled to feel proud, too, because this wasn't the Scottish Cup final where we had let our fans and ourselves down. This was a game where, even though we lost, we regained our pride.

As we punished Barcelona and Borussia on the break, Gothenburg punished us with a marvellously struck goal by Lennart Nilsson. Billy Thomson had absolutely no chance, the ball going along the inside of the side net so closely that there were people trying to say it had actually gone in that way. It hadn't. It was the perfect shot.

We now had three goals to score to win – but, you know, I believed that was possible, right up to minutes from the end.

As our pride came back, so did our ability and we stretched a team which is outstanding in Europe. In fact after John Clark scored a magnificent equaliser on the night for us – how a big man like him could turn so gracefully and direct one of his special 'bending' shots so accurately still amazes me – they definitely wilted.

If we had got one more then, we would have won the UEFA Cup, and the season that collapsed so terribly around us would have been a great season. But football is built on 'if's' and if they aren't in your favour, that's it . . .

As a final point, let me mention our supporters. They grew through the season: from being great, to being absolutely magnificent.

While football is still worried in many places about hooliganism, about bad crowd behaviour, they proved there is still a huge army of real football followers about. People who love the game and truly enjoy watching it. People who will even see their team beaten and give the opposition deserved applause.

We went back out to thank them after the game, our manager had to go out even later to plead with them to go home – at the same time thanking them for their support.

But the really impressive reaction came from the Gothenburg players and officials. They went to parade the Cup to their fans and found they were also being cheered for their performance and success by our fans.

They admitted at the end that, at first, they couldn't believe it, but that after they did, they had never felt so good.

I desperately wanted Dundee United to win both the Scottish Cup and the UEFA Cup. I would even have settled for one of the trophies. However we ended that roller coaster season without any major honours.

But in the seasons ahead I believe our turn for the silverware and the flags will come again . . .

Meantime, let's get back to where and when it all began –

3

The World's Smallest Sweeper

Portsmouth manager Alan Ball doesn't know me from Adam.

We haven't met, I haven't seen him play other than on television – but he was my hero when he played and any success I have had in the game must be partly down to him.

I'll explain.

Back when he was at his peak I was playing for my Edinburgh school, St Anthony's.

And I must have been the smallest sweeper in the world! I was 12 years of age and, pulling myself to my full height, measured exactly 4ft 8 ins from the ground to the top of my head.

Make no mistake, it was a great team and I was proud to be in it, but I was so small . . .

Then I saw Alan Ball play in a game on television.

Though he wasn't as small as me he was, like me, outreached by several inches by the players around him, in his own team as well as the opposition.

Even at that age I had firm beliefs and one of them was that, no matter how small you were, if you worked hard and refused to accept lack of height as a handicap, you could make it in the game.

Watching him playing at the very peak of English football with Everton and Arsenal and, in particular, with England in the 1966 World Cup, proved I was right.

Opponents could tackle him, try to use their physical advantages, but they could never put him out of the game. What he lacked in stature he made up for in tremendous spirit, a total refusal to accept he was ever beaten.

The classic case was the 1966 World Cup final at Wembley.

Schnellinger, the West German full back, was huge by comparison with Ball – and he didn't stand on ceremony when he tackled. But that didn't count by the end of the game. He had been run ragged by my hero.

Maybe I am biased, but, despite great performances from many players in both teams in that game, I thought it was the 'Alan Ball factor' more than any other which saw England finally come out on top.

As I look back on my career, I never regret being so small as a young lad. It appears to me that, being small, you have more to prove and set about proving it with greater determination than normal-sized people. In later life, no matter your physical stature, that determination stands you in good stead.

I have friends who played with and against me as a youngster and who are taller and perhaps better players, too. None of them made it at senior level. Could it be that they 'peaked' as youngsters? That because of their stature they didn't keep putting in that extra bit of effort smaller players had to put in?

I know that can't be all of it – some just drifted away from the game or didn't fancy the disciplines of professional football. But I feel certain it was a contributory factor.

I was born in Edinburgh's General Hospital on July 25, 1954. I'm not afraid to give the date. I believe it is an honour and an achievement to be in the game well into your thirties and don't understand players who suddenly start getting all coy about their age once they get over their mid-twenties.

Let's face it, those that matter, team managers and the like know exactly how old you are any time your name crops up. They have the records.

My first clear recollection of life is being dared to jump on to the step behind a moving baker's van, doing it and getting a right verbal roasting from both Mum and Dad. Mum has always said I had an angelic face as a youngster – but not the temperament to go with it! As I was two-and-a-half at the time of the van incident I take her point.

My first home was a prefab in Redhall, only a few miles from Tynecastle, home of Hearts. My father, Jimmy, was a postman, my mother's name is Betty and I have a brother Kevin and a sister Colette. We moved to Juniper Green because Dad was posted (!) there when I was about four and my parents still live there.

I was small all the way up to my teens, knock-kneed, thin-legged. Just about everything, in fact, you wouldn't expect a future footballer to be. Right from the very start, though, a footballer is what I was determined to be – which is where lucky breaks come in.

I'm the one who DIDN'T start by kicking the ball against a wall . . . although I did my share of that on occasion.

I started on a surface that can only be compared to Wembley at its best. Other folk called it the drying green, where the Mums from our corner hung out their washing.

To me it was Hampden and Wembley rolled into one.

At its worst the grass surface was very good; when my father carefully cut it with the mower the surface was perfect for playing football on, the posts holding up the washing lines perfect as goalposts.

They could have played Scotland v. England on that patch of grass and even the greatest players would have gone away raving about it.

Kevin was four years older than me and many an hour we spent out there playing our own version of classic games of the past. He didn't fancy losing, though, and as I gradually got better and better because I never stopped practising, he would 'do a Bill Shankly'.

That was, decide the game was over when I threatened to win or keep it going until he got the winning goal.

We also played 'shapes'. Here you had to hit a certain area of the wall with the ball. Easy? Not our way. It was one touch.

This meant if the ball ran off down the road you had to catch it, and control and hit it against the target area in one go.

The more I played, the more I wanted to play football. I was never interested in anything else. I didn't read comics, I read football magazines like *Goal.* I lived for the game.

My first real break into it came when I was at St Cuthbert's R.C. Primary School in Slateford – class of '59, to put it the American way.

I got into the team as a striker. George Lavery, Ronnie Tennant, Stuart Cunningham, Brian Hart – he laid the carpet in my present house in Monifieth – were all in the team. I'll never forget them because they were among my first real team-mates, but the years have rolled on and we have mostly lost touch.

My first manager was a woman teacher, Miss Veronica Laidlaw, with school janitor Bob Stuart helping. At eight years young I was playing against lads of ten and eleven – and they gave me no breaks because I was younger and much smaller.

Not that I wanted them, as I said earlier. I believed I was good enough to be there and never stopped trying to prove it.

The most important thing about that first team, though, was that both Miss Laidlaw and Mr Stuart were disciplinarians. They insisted things be done a certain way and woe betide you if they weren't.

There are people who say we are severely disciplined at

Tannadice. So what? Isn't life about discipline, especially in a team game? And isn't self-discipline essential in any walk of life?

Believe me I haven't suffered any under the discipline imposed by manager Jim McLean on the United players, but then I had a tremendous start in that very first team.

Actually, Miss Laidlaw is headmistress of my old school now and I had the pleasure of meeting her recently when I did a prize-giving ceremony to the various teams in several sports. I had the cheek to say, 'Hello Veronica'. I'd never have risked that in the old days!

Another privilege I had when I played for St Cuthbert's is that we played at Meggetland. What that means to youngsters in the Edinburgh area is that we were actually competing with goal-nets at each end.

To this day I believe one of the greatest moments in any footballer's life is his first experience of goal-nets. Instead of the ball running on and on or someone 'fielding' it, it hits the back of the net which leaps with the force of the shot or header. It is a tremendous feeling to see that when you are the scorer.

I also learned something else at Meggetland. That all the good players in the world weren't in my school team. For instance, Hunters Tryst had a lad called Eric Carruthers. He was what was called an inside forward in those days and he really could play. His blonde hair and his skill marked him out in every game. Although the promise didn't fully flower, he went to Hearts and was, in fact, there at the same time as my brother Kevin.

And it is about time I said more about big brother, or he will never forgive me.

Dad played a bit of football in the RAF, my uncle Hugh had a couple of trials with Celtic, but there is no family history of professional football until Kevin, and then me.

Kevin went to St Cuthbert's, then St Andrews, but while my Dad let me get on with my football fever he insisted that Kevin serve an apprenticeship.

He did, as a printer, and now works at his trade with the Standard Life Assurance Company, but the football skill he possessed saw him become one of the most travelled players of all.

That old joke about having more clubs than Jack Nicklaus applies as much to Kevin as it does to the man who claims he first said it – former Scotland boss Tommy Docherty.

A good young player with Salvesen Boys' Club, Kevin was signed by John Prentice when he was manager of Falkirk – that's the same

John Prentice who started Jim McLean on the way to the top when he managed Dundee, and the present United manager was his coach, by the way.

Freed after a year, Kevin joined junior club Haddington. Hearts spotted him and he had a really tremendous first season with them under Bobby Seith, now a chiropodist in Dundee and who regularly covers Tannadice games for BBC radio.

His partnership with Donald Ford, that magnificent footballer/ cricketer who, in my opinion, didn't get the international recognition he deserved, was definitely special.

Then, suddenly, Kevin's play wasn't all it had been and he was off again on his travels. To Carlisle, to East Fife, to Morton, to East Fife again, to Dunfermline, to Berwick, to Falkirk.

I genuinely admire him for his perseverance. There is many a footballer who, once he is freed by a club, simply gives up on the game.

Kevin didn't. He kept on trying, giving the game all he had. It didn't work out, but he didn't give up.

It is easy to be a player when you are at the top. When you get knocked back again and again like he was and still stick at it, it says a tremendous amount for your strength of character.

Before I leave the early days, when it all started happening for me, I would like to bring in one other team – the all-conquering St Anthony's for whom I had the privilege of playing when we did what was considered impossible. In the 1967-69 period, we swept the boards in schools football.

Inspired by the brilliant coaching of P.E. teacher George Brough, who had played for Hibs and Stirling Albion, and the management of technical master John Halliday, we were Scottish schools champions three years in succession. Nothing was too much trouble for these two, no detail was overlooked. They worked like my present boss Jim McLean works, unendingly, to make their team the best and got their just reward when we were – again and again.

We won the Under-13 Edinburgh Shield and Cup and national championship; the Under-14 Shield and Cup and national title; the Under-15 Shield and Cup and Scottish Intermediate Shield. It was incredible.

We played 79 games, were beaten in only two. Scored 433 goals, conceded only 50 and I immodestly treasure the cutting from the *Daily Express* of May, 1969, which says, 'Pride of the side is skipper Paul Hegarty, 14, the smallest man in the team. He stands just 5 ft

1 ins tall but is reckoned one of the finest midfield players in the district'.

Thanks for the memories to such as Gordon Knowles, Mark Williamson, Gavin Hancock, Alex Wright, John McMullen, Alex McNulty, Jim Love, Alan Gordon, Joe Phair, Steve Hancock, Richard O'Rourke, Mike Devlin, Jim Flanagan.

Winning every competition open to you at secondary school level over a three-year period is a record we can all be proud of forever.

4

Signed by Lisbon Lion

I am often asked why, as an Edinburgh lad, I started my senior career with Hamilton Academicals, which, when you put it that way, sounds more like the name of a rugby rather than a football team.

There is a very simple answer.

They were the only ones who asked me.

I trained every Tuesday at Tynecastle. I hoped they'd put me on an 'S' form, but it never happened. I heard about interest from Celtic, from all sorts of clubs, but it never went beyond paper talk as far as I was concerned.

Dave Johnstone was a scout for Hamilton. He asked me to play in a trial game for Accies. Their manager, not long appointed and not long to remain in the job, was Ronnie Simpson.

Now that was special. Like just about every young lad in Scotland at that time, the Lisbon Lions of Celtic, the men who took the European Cup to Britain for the first time under the management of Jock Stein and captaincy of Billy McNeill, were the No.1 team to me.

And here I was actually being given a chance by the goalkeeper of that team – Ronnie Simpson. I played my heart out and was signed. My ambition was achieved. I had made it into senior football.

But before I leave the Lisbon Lions, let me make another point.

There were many great players in that team, but my particular hero is one who didn't often get the headlines – John Clark. To me he was the same as the man I was so often to play alongside in the years ahead, Dave Narey.

Nothing flash, got on with the job – and was always there when it mattered. In the case of Clark there was also the fact that he was a smaller player than many around him, but, like Alan Ball, never knew when he was beaten, commanded his part of the park.

Now back to Hamilton. In chairman Jan Stepek they had a man with ambition and, even as an 18-year-old I reasoned that this, allied to the fact they were bottom of the Second Division, meant there was only one way the club could go . . . UP.

I was a part-timer working with the Scottish Widows Insurance

Company in Edinburgh, a 9 to 5 job in the New Business Input department.

Looking back makes me wonder if young players today get it too easy.

I trained three times a week and, accompanied by team-mate Frannie McGann, got the train from Edinburgh to Glasgow, walked from Queen Street to Central Station, got another train for Hamilton, arrived at 6.45, started training at 7pm.

Once training was finished it was the same in reverse with us getting home about midnight and having been up since around eight in the morning.

It wasn't all that pleasant especially in the winter, but I was into professional football and nothing was going to stop me being a success.

It wasn't long before Billy Lamont took over from Ronnie Simpson, then it was Eric Smith, a very professional manager who had been schooled at Celtic and Leeds and really knew the game.

My wages were a basic of £8 plus £10 a point. That doesn't sound much but if you were in a League Cup section in which you played a couple of times a week and won, the result was an income of between £40 and £50 that week.

Put on top of £12 in my job with the Scottish Widows, you are talking about a top of around £60 a week, relative riches at that time.

Many things happened to me at Hamilton, apart from beginning to make my name in the game as 'this exciting new striker', 'a striker with a great future in the game', 'a newcomer with a marvellous eye for a goal chance' to quote some reports of the time.

First of all I started to stretch.

I was 5 ft 3 ins when I was 16, from 16 to 18 I edged up to between 5 ft 5 ins and 5 ft 6 ins. Then at eighteen, nineteen and twenty, when with Accies, I grew to 5 ft 10½ inches, which I am now. It is still not big for a centre-half, my position for most of my time with Dundee United, but I have always been blessed with the ability to get well up for high balls, so it hasn't been a drawback.

I have never really practised heading, it seems to have been a talent that has been there all my life.

I took stick at work if Hamilton lost, especially off Isobel (Issy) Strachan, but it is what you expect in this game.

Another work-mate was Colin McIsaac, and thereby hangs a tale of my first car.

A few wins under the belt at Hamilton and I had a bob or two to spare. I'd have liked a Rolls Royce, I still would (!), but had to settle for a 1958 – that was fourteen years old at that time – Morris Minor that Arthur Negus would have been pleased to describe in his antique show on television.

The seller – Colin McIsaac. The price £50. The relationship between me and that car was a love-hate one. I loved it when it got us through to Hamilton in one go instead of having all that train journey, I hated it when it let me down, which, to be fair, it didn't do often.

I had company on my journeys in team-mate Tam Stevens. We took turn about to journey in my car or his – but I must say I preferred mine. Maybe it was small, but his was ridiculous. A Honda, so tiny that I often wished I was 4 ft 8 ins again.

Its only saving grace was that it seemed to do about 3000 miles to the gallon, great stuff when you're watching the pennies.

I had many happy days at Hamilton and we had good players like Ricky Ferguson, still with the club, Gordon Hamilton, whom I bumped into not long ago when I was heading for Belgium with Scotland Under 21's (I was an over-age player in case you are wondering ... considerably over-age), Phil Bonnyman, Jimmy Brand, Jackie McInally, father of Celtic's Alan, Arthur McMillan (club captain) and Drew Young.

There was also the unforgettable voice of Fergie – who is, I believe, no longer welcome at Douglas Park. I could hear him shouting no matter how much noise there was from elsewhere in the ground. While I was at Hamilton it was praise, nowadays it is anything but.

I was a striker at Hamilton and, the record shows, a pretty good one: 30 goals in 99 games spread over two-and-a-bit seasons added to a good number of assists isn't at all bad.

I achieved my first aim in the game by joining Accies as a professional, but two games in particular and one player in particular proved to me there was a long way to go before I could consider I was playing at the top club level.

The first game was against Leeds United at Douglas Park. It was a friendly arranged because of Eric Smith's continuing contact with the man who masterminded Leeds, Don Revie.

It wasn't the full Leeds team that was, at the time, the most feared outfit in England and one of the outstanding teams in Europe.

It was, though, a very strong line-up, featuring players like Gary Sprake, the Welsh international goalkeeper; Paul Reaney, the

England full back; Terry Yorath, another Welsh internationalist, plus three Scots.

They were Peter Lorimer, the Dundee-born winger-striker who had one of the hardest shots the game has ever seen; Frank Gray, brother of the then better-known Eddie, but who was to go on and win many caps for Scotland as a full back himself; and the one and only Joe Jordan, that lion of a centre-forward who led Scotland so often, not least when we qualified for the World Cup with his goal against Wales at Anfield.

That was almost ten years ago now and still the argument rages whether he headed or hand-balled the vital goal.

Some team . . . yet we beat them 4-3 in front of a crowd of 10,000, at least six times our normal at Douglas Park.

The adrenalin flowed that night, I'll tell you. I can remember it as clearly as if it was yesterday, although it was, in fact, in August, 1973.

My striking partner at Hamilton was Neil Hood. Usually he did the hard work and I stuck the ball in the net! This time the roles were reversed – I laid on two goals and was flattered to read in the *Daily Record* next day, 'Accies football was a revelation and they had the classiest player on the field in Paul Hegarty, teenage brother of East Fife star Kevin'.

But it was Neil who got the goals – three of them. Brilliant.

We were actually 4-1 up with 18 minutes to go, but then I found out the difference between full-time and part-time training.

As we steadily ran out of steam they got stronger and stronger. Arthur Mann, formerly with Hearts, pulled one back and, six minutes from time, Lorimer blasted home a penalty.

Our other scorer was Jim Brand, theirs Mick Bates. The teams were: Hamilton – MacLean; Frew, McKernon; Hamilton, Gillespie, Bonnyman; Young, Scott, Hood, Hegarty, Brand. Subs – Whiteside, McMillan, Fairley, McArthur. Leeds – Sprake; Reaney, Hampton; Yorath, Ellam, F. Gray; Lorimer, Bates, Jordan, Mann, Liddell. Subs – Shaw, McGinlay, O'Neill.

Then there was a home and away League Cup tie against Celtic and one other game against Celtic, which allowed me to be on the park with one of the all-time greats.

The League Cup tie ended 6-2 on aggregate. Kenny Dalglish was beginning to make his name, Billy McNeill was there, Danny McGrain, too, as well as Jimmy Bone, now assistant manager of St Mirren, whom we met in the Scottish Cup final of 1986-87.

It wasn't so much the players as the incredible atmosphere

The Year is 1979 and it's all smiles as Ray Stewart and I do a Dundee United double. Ray won the Scottish Professional Footballers Association Young Player of the Year award and I was Player of the Year.

Back home Linda and I proudly display the same Player of the Year trophy – not that young Paul was too impressed!

The Hegarty threesome – sister Colette, me and older brother Kevin.

An up-to-date picture taken for the book – me and wife Linda with sons Christopher, Paul and Mark.

St Cuthbert's R.C. Primary School team. I'm third from left, front row, holding our first trophy. Back left is janitor Bob Stewart, our joint team boss, along with Veronica Laidlaw (right).

And here's me, dwarfed by the trophies won by the all-conquering St Anthony's Secondary School team.

As John Wark (right) and Alan Hansen (6) look on anxiously, I clear a ball in a challenge with Argentine striker Luque. An international match played in 1979.

Chasing a ball with two Argentinians ... but the man that matters is in the background – Diego Maradona, the player I rate the greatest.

My first senior team – Hamilton Accies. From left (back) – Bobby Reid, physiotherapist; Jim Brand, Ricky McClunie, Frank Grant, Jimmy O'Reilly, Ricardo Ferguson, Paul Hegarty, Danny Smith, Neil Hood, Jamie Fairlie, Pat Barclay, coach; (front) – Andy Lawless, Jackie McInally, George Hunter, Gordon Hamilton, Ian Campbell, Jim Frew, Pat McGrogan, Eric Smith, manager.

Tug o' war between Bobby Glennie, the Dundee captain, and myself, the United captain, before our teams met in the League Cup final.

Beating Derek Johnstone in the air in a Rangers game – and that wasn't easy! Ray Stewart is on the right and, behind him, Davie Cooper, a lot heavier than in recent years, I'd say.

A quartet of United internationalists – Richard Gough, me, Paul Sturrock and Dave Narey. Since then, of course, Eamonn Bannon, Maurice Malpas, Jim McInally and Ian Redford have all been with Scotland, and Billy Thomson had international honours before he joined us from St Mirren.

With Scotland in a Largs get-together. I am third from the right in a front row also featuring Danny McGrain, Gordon Strachan and Kenny Dalglish.

The 55th game in Europe for No. 5 – me – and as Paul Sturrock (centre) and Ralph Milne hold up the jerseys, I'm keeping a tight grip on my Personality of the Month bottle!

I'm obviously slightly chuffed at scoring a semi-final goal against Celtic – and Paul Sturrock (left) and Davie Dodds are no less pleased.

Displaying the Premier League trophy win in season 1982-83 before the first game of the following season – from left (back) – Dodds, Taylor, Clark, McAlpine, Holt, Narey, Gough, Stark, who was tragically put out of the game with injury; (front) – Milne, Hegarty, Kirkwood, Malpas, Bannon.

The team 'chair' me and the League Cup after our first win – from left – Phillips, Narey, Payne, Kopel, me, McAlpine, Dodds, Pettigrew, Sturrock, Bannon.

Jim McLean, my manager at Tannadice.

Chaired by fans after our first League Cup triumph against Aberdeen.

Getting the low down on a dangerous cross ball against Manchester United in the UEFA Cup. Also grounded are keeper Hamish McAlpine and, on the right, Norman Whiteside.

Scoring a goal against Celtic despite the close attention of Roy Aitken.

surrounding them that got to me. They were with a big club, they knew it, their supporters knew it and believed in them. The whole thing was another dimension to me, a part-time player with a Second Division club. I wanted to get involved at that level.

Later came the privilege of being on the park with the all-time great . . . Celtic winger Jimmy Johnstone.

To this day I can't recall the score or much about the game – other than the Johnstone performance.

By this time, I had played against some good players, seen many others in action live and on television. This one, though, was incredible.

When he got the ball he looked just another player you could walk in and take it off. He'd show our defenders the ball, they'd wade in for it – and he would be gone, yards away in the blink of an eye. They'd try stalking him, ganging up on him, but when that ball was at his feet it was his until he decided to get rid of it.

There and then I realised that, though I had made it into professional football, I had a long way to go to reach the level where I could compete with that sort of talent and expect to at least break even.

[illegible]

What had I done wrong? [illegible]

[illegible] worked hard at training and in every game.

Still, it was a lesson.

Take nothing for granted in life. [illegible] Always be prepared for upsets.

[illegible]

5

Shock Sacking

Football is an emotional game. In the heat of the moment you can say things and do things you regret afterwards. It has happened to me as I explain elsewhere, but there have been two things happen to me which weren't in the heat of the moment, but which still hurt, yet also taught me, in the first case in particular, a valuable lesson in life.

I was at a coaching course recently and met Kenny Brown, from Edinburgh.

He said his brother was asking for me, and I would have been a hypocrite if I had returned the compliment!

His brother is Ian 'Boobs' Brown, who was in charge of Edinburgh's Salvesen Boys' Club, with whom I played for around four years up until I was 17.

Everything had been going well for me in football. My ambition was to be a professional and things were heading the right way as I progressed through St Cuthbert's and St Anthony's schools and with Salvesen.

I would have liked to have been taller, but otherwise I was on course.

Then, out of the blue as far as I was concerned, I was called in to see 'Boobs' and told he was letting me go.

I was sixteen, it was the first real setback of my life. I couldn't believe it at first and when it finally sank in that I really wasn't wanted I was close to tears.

What had I done wrong? Had my play suddenly fallen apart? My world had, but I couldn't get an answer and still don't know to this day what it was.

If he fancied other players could do my job in the team better than me, fair enough. But I'd like to have known. I gave everything to football, worked hard at training and in every game.

Still, it was a lesson.

Take nothing for granted in life. Never think things are going smoothly. Always be prepared for upsets.

I left Salvesen for Tynecastle Boys' Club with many happy

memories behind me, but for that one exception which, to this day, still bugs me.

Then there was my departure from Hamilton for Dundee United.

Manager Eric Smith, with whom I had had a good relationship, had a real go at me when I left.

There were headings like 'Storm as Hegarty leaves Hamilton' and they were based on Eric's comments.

AFTER he had sold me he lashed out with, 'This has to be said. I am disgusted at Paul Hegarty's attitude over the past month. He has been most unreasonable.

'His fellow professionals in the team feel let down. I worked hard to keep this player and the club did not want to sell him.'

Let me make a few points clear.

My fellow professionals at Hamilton never let ME know anything about feeling let down. I'm still friends with them.

And I don't think the manager allowed for the pressure that was on me at that time.

Regularly in the newspapers I read of players being watched by this, that and the other club.

If you are an experienced professional this is bound to get through to you, but imagine what it is like when you are, like I was at that time, a part-time pro who was scoring goals regularly and had the burning ambition to progress in the game.

I read names like Celtic, Hull City, Leeds United, Airdrie, Hearts, Aberdeen, Southend and Sunderland being linked with mine. Some were big clubs, full-time, trophy-winners. Everything I wanted.

But I did not do anything like playing to get away.

What happened was that, with all the comment I lost a bit of concentration and my game suffered.

My reply to the manager at the time, and I still stand by it was 'I have been below form recently because all the talk of transfers was affecting me'.

'Nothing was deliberate and I will always be grateful to Mr Smith for the help he has given me.'

That was said as I moved on to Dundee United and the full-time football I craved.

I now know a lot more about the game than I did and wonder if the situation was that the club didn't want it to appear that they were too eager to get rid of a player who was getting goals.

To counter any criticism in this direction an insistence that the player had wanted away was probably considered in order –

although it didn't do much for the player!

Incidentally, the figure quoted again and again at the time as my transfer fee was £40,000. In fact it was £27,500.

Whatever, I prefer to remember the happier times with both Salvesen and Hamilton, and in this direction cherish a letter I received from a Mr Boyle, from East Kilbride, on joining Dundee United.

He wrote, 'I should like to take this opportunity of writing to you and congratulating you on your signing for Dundee United.

'My son who is thirteen (this was written in November, 1974) and I have followed Hamilton Accies for a long time now and have watched your progress with pleasure.

'We will continue to do so even though you have departed the Douglas Park scene.

'I should like to thank you for the entertainment you have given both of us in your time at Hamilton and I know that this first step to Dundee will herald an outstanding career in football.

'With your ability and endeavour there are no limits to your horizons and I look forward to reading of your future progress.

Every possible good wish. Sincerely . . .'

Football has its highs and its lows.

That sort of letter can make up for an awful lot of lows.

Mind you, Hamilton doesn't only mean football to me. It was while I was with the Accies that I really met my wife-to-be Linda.

By 'really' I mean that I had known her before through the church, but in the way of any youngster obsessed as I was with football she was just a girl and not that important because, let's face it, she didn't play football and didn't seem all that interested in it.

It was really Frannie McGann who started it – for which I now thank him!

Dancing never really interested me, but his patter must have been really good on this occasion because he talked me into going to a disco.

Not only that, he told me during the disco that we had been invited to a party after the dancing . . . in a house in Morningside.

Now you have to understand that, at that time, Scottish Television had a programme called 'Scotsport' running. It showed a game every weekend and I watched and absorbed every move in that game.

I still had burning ambition to get to the top in the game, and watching the best players made me realise how far I had to go. Not that I lacked confidence. Often my reasoning was more along the lines of, 'I could play for them, I'm good enough'.

But back to the night of the party. And while I have thanked Frannie McGann here I must apologise to Arthur Montford. He was the match commentator – and on the night of the party I missed him.

Yes, McGann talked me into going. Nothing flash about our arrival either. We got a bus which deposited us not too far from the house and walked the rest of the way.

I am no John Travolta, but I did my share of dancing and suddenly noticed Linda. I asked her to dance, and that was the beginning of our relationship.

From then on it was a steady increase in courting and, finally, marriage, three years later. Marrying LInda was the best move I've ever made. She has always been very supportive and understanding, something I regard as essential as in our line of work you have your fair share of ups and downs, which affects the family.

Linda admits to not being really impressed with football at the start, even though she was brought up with two brothers, Kenneth and Stephen. But nowadays she loves the game and goes to most home matches.

We now have three more ardent fans – our children Paul (8), Mark (6) and Christopher (3). The two oldest boys go to most games along with Linda's Dad and brother. My own parents used to be regular supporters until my Dad took ill a few years back. Linda's Mum is a stay-at-home supporter where she usually is babysitting for us.

I am still as keen on the game as I was, make no mistake, but the difference is that I allow time for other things now, mostly to do with our family.

I've been fortunate there too. I appreciate the upbringing my parents, Jimmy and Betty Hegarty, gave me and, unlike so many people, if you are to believe comedians (!), I have great in-laws in Jimmy and Effie Higgins. We are like one big family.

Mentioning family reminds me of one of the few times I felt really annoyed with the media.

Mark was born the day before the Cup final against Rangers back in 1981 when we drew 0-0 first game and lost 4-1 in the replay. Linda was taken to hospital on Thursday to await the baby's arrival. Mark was born on Friday afternoon. I was in a deep sleep when the phone range at midnight. It was a reporter phoning to ask if the baby had been born yet!

I have always found the media to be good to work with if you co-operate and I have always tried to do just that. On this occasion, though, I confess I forgot myself and had a few harsh words to say. I hope you find that understandable ... and, incidentally, I hardly got to sleep again that night.

6

Jim McLean

When I signed for Dundee United in November, 1974, I did so on a blank contract.

Why? Because I had, from the moment I first met him, complete trust in the honesty of the man who signed me, my manager for the past thirteen years, Jim McLean.

I know this man as well as any player in the land, yet do I know him? I often wonder.

What I definitely do is respect his 'magic' as a manager/coach, his unbelievable knowledge of the game and that honesty I talked about at the start.

Going back to the beginning of what has been the major part of my life up to now, I had read and heard of club after club being interested in me and about to bid.

Like it was when I signed for Hamilton, however, Dundee United were the club that came in with a bid which turned out to be acceptable to Accies and which took me to Tayside.

Billy Lamont, assistant at Hamilton, had told me to be patient, to persevere and the break I wanted would come. History has proved him right as far as Dundee United are concerned.

Then came the word that I had to see United manager Jim McLean. The meeting place was arranged as the motorway cafe at Harthill, halfway between Edinburgh and Glasgow.

As my brother Kevin was a professional and knew the ropes about signing things and talking terms, I asked if he would come along with me. He immediately said 'Yes'.

I suppose if Jim McLean – and me for that matter – sat at a table in that cafe now the autograph hunters would be round us in double quick time, certainly round him after what has happened over the past few years.

But then United weren't all that good a team, not well publicised, and he was not far into his managerial career. So the few folk that were about didn't spare us a second glance.

I felt like stopping some of them saying, 'I'm getting my chance of full-time football, my dream is going to come true.' But even at that, they would probably have said 'Oh?' and moved on.

The talks didn't take long. My manager-to-be said he wanted me to join him at Tannadice, that he was prepared to pay what Hamilton Accies wanted by way of a fee.

He went on, 'It won't be a holiday camp. There will be discipline.'

He then advised me of the terms he was offering and told me to go and chat about it with my brother.

I said, 'What do you think?'

Kevin replied, 'He's straight. Give it a bash.'

I didn't hesitate. I went back to the table, said 'I'd like to sign', did so on a blank form and shook hands.

One month later I was handed my first contract. Every single thing that had been agreed verbally was down in black and white. The feelings of my brother and myself that we were dealing with a genuinely honest man were proved 100 per cent correct.

I started with United on a basic wage of £45 a week. But that wasn't the important thing. What was important was that I had achieved my goal of becoming a full-time player with a First Division Club who, like Hamilton when I joined them, were going only one way . . . UP.

As I will explain shortly, I can't say I have never regretted one moment of my time at Tannadice, but I am in no doubt now that the decision I took those years ago was the right one.

As for the discipline, it is strict, but that is only as it should be, and hadn't I had the proper grounding in this direction with my school teams?

Actually, on the discipline angle I have one proud boast about my years with United.

There are fines for turning up late for training, for not doing what you should do at training, for having dirty boots – they can vary between £5 and £10.

I have never been fined for any of those things.

In fact the only time I have been involved in this side of things is when we beat Motherwell 6–0: the manager felt we didn't entertain enough and held back £50 of our entertainment bonus.

There were big headlines after that about 'McLean Fines Players After 6–0 Win' and so on, but, in fact, it wasn't a fine, it was non-payment of money we had to earn by entertaining. That is very different.

So I haven't been fined for anything!

I'll tell you one thing he is 'death' on. Being sent off for retaliation.

He can't understand the stupidity of that and, I confess, neither can I.

Another thing neither he nor I are into is alcoholic drink. He is a teetotaller, I am very close, though I don't mind a glass of wine with a meal or the odd glass of beer. Let's put it another way. If the landlord of my local depended on the manager and me for his income, he would go bankrupt in a matter of weeks.

Football is a physically demanding sport and is getting more so every season. The days when you could have a few bevvies and go out and play – like we are always hearing they used to do in 'the old days' – are gone.

Some players might kid themselves on that they can do it, but at the very least it shortens their career, at the worst it means they simply don't have a career.

So if you want to be a player at the top level, lay off the drink. It has no place in any athlete's preparation for his job.

7

Torn to Shreds

I touched on my earliest experience of manager Jim McLean when I told you of his honesty over the first contract I signed with United. That was plain sailing. It hasn't always been that way between him and me – or between him and most players.

I don't say that in any harsh way. The longer I play, the more I know about the game and the more I realise how difficult a manager's job is, and how many things he has to take into consideration while the individual player is, equally naturally, concerned with his career and his life.

Summarising the man I would say this.

He has a truly exceptional football brain, his views on the game, which he seems to think about all the time, are precise and to the point, and his putting over his ideas, his coaching, second to none.

That comes over particularly strongly in his half-time talks – which can be shouting matches – in the dressing room.

It's his overall awareness of every aspect of football which is so impressive. Big issues or small, nothing escapes his attention.

It shows in things like the players he signs. He studies their ability in detail, knows exactly what he can make of them in the context of Dundee United. That isn't all, though. He also studies their character before he signs them, finds out all about them and their behaviour off the field as much as on it.

Do they behave themselves? Drink? Smoke? Gamble? Are they reasonable? Will they rock the boat?

The people he has signed since I have been at Tannadice have conformed to a pattern – and it isn't a bad pattern at that.

There hasn't been one bad or vicious newcomer, one who would upset the balance, cause trouble around him.

There have been ambitious players – Richard Gough was ambitious to move on to a bigger club and finally went to Tottenham Hotspur. But I am not knocking that. After all, in my way I was ambitious to join a club playing in a bigger theatre when I moved from Hamilton Accies to United. I haven't regretted that, and I'm sure Richard won't regret his move to Spurs.

The blend is right with United and that is down to the Boss. He has signed or groomed the players, and it shows he knows what he is doing that we have had success.

His blend on the field is achieved with a mixture of shouting at some players and coaxing others.

Footballers like to be told now and again where they are going wrong, and he has proved that his methods work.

That proof comes in our record of winning the Premier League title and the League Cup, our runs in Europe and, at an individual level, the number of caps for their country won by United players . . . don't forget that there had been no Scotland honours for United players until he got his ideas to work and produced the teams which have won success.

The type of player he likes is one with individual skill and the ability to work hard at improving himself. He works his way round their weaknesses and plays on their strengths.

I arrived at Tannadice as a striker, pretty satisfied with myself on account of the goals I had been getting with Hamilton Accies. And I got a rude awakening!

The first month after joining the club I seemed never to see a day pass but I was in his office. He was always moaning at me. 'What kind of performances are you giving me?' was the theme of most of our (one-sided) talks. He was always looking for better things, more for the £27,500 the club had paid for me.

Some of the comments he made to a youngster who had come from a part-time club with stars in his eyes, believing he had achieved his life's ambition, were upsetting – and that's a very mild word for my feelings.

How would you like to be told things like 'you are nothing' when you thought you were doing not badly at all and were certainly giving all you had?

I got to the stage where I honestly wondered what I was doing here and if I had made the right decision.

Kevin had warned me that he was a disciplinarian, but I had never in any way been ready for this sort of treatment.

With a part-time club you are involved, but it isn't the be-all and end-all of your life. There is the job you have outside the game. It takes the pressure off the football as football takes the pressure off the other work.

Now, football was my life. All of it. And I was being told I wasn't all that good at what I was doing.

I was in digs with Paul Sturrock and Tom McAdam. When you have a wife and family, or when you are living in the family environment in which you have been brought up, you can discuss your personal feelings with people who understand you and your problems. But we were probably all in the same boat and didn't want to let one another know!

A lot depends on the individual when this is happening to you. To be honest, it still gets to me. You are doing your best and someone is saying your best is not good enough. Criticism is hard to take in any walk of life. I think footballers take it less well than most.

Getting a bollocking and being torn to shreds isn't flavour of the month, no matter how laid back you are – and with my ambition to do well as a player I wasn't all that laid back!

Having said all that, let me get my conclusion on the man down clearly.

With my experience in the game as it stands now, I realise what was being done to me was for my own good. I had come as a centre forward, a striker, but he was not convinced that was my best position. He had to make me change my approach, my game, he had to find out what I was best at, partly because of the money spent, partly because he wouldn't have spent it if he hadn't thought I had the ability to be part of his plans for Dundee United.

So, in the midst of all the shouting and criticism, I found myself in practice games moving back to midfield, moving out wide, moving even further back.

I was playing alongside Andy Gray, very shortly to move to Aston Villa for a massive £100,000 fee, and the general impression was that I had been bought to cover his inevitable departure.

I suppose I thought that, too, at the time . . . but now I realise there were other ideas in the Boss's mind.

I played 99 games for Accies and scored 30 goals. I set off for United with only 11 games that first season, plus eight substitutions, and scored four goals. Next season it was 40 games (twice substitute) and 11 goals.

I have always been honest with myself about my game, and what I was finding was that though goals had flowed pretty regularly for Accies, along with a steady supply of assists, I was now in the big league and lacked that wee bit extra pace you needed to be a top striker at the top level.

It was only a half-yard, but it was the difference between getting to the ball in front of the defender or just after him. That delay meant you looked always as though you were struggling and the crowd were quick to spot that and slow to welcome me.

To be honest, when it actually happened that I went back to centre half it didn't take me long to realise that at last I had found my real position, facing play, defending instead of attacking.

I remember Gordon Strachan, who is with Manchester United after his spells with Dundee and Aberdeen and is one of the cleverest players Scotland has ever produced, saying once, 'It is easier to destroy than to create'. He is right – up to a point. What I have found, though, is that you can create from a defensive position after you have broken up, or destroyed if you like, an opposition attack.

Sometime, in emergencies, it has to be the big 'hoof' up the park the way you are looking, but I don't think I'll get any argument when I say that we at United often build very effective attacks from what started as defensive situations.

Getting back to Jim McLean, his attitude to a player can be summed up in something I once heard him say.

'You think I moan and shout a lot at you. It's when I stop moaning and shouting at you that you should start worrying.'

So the moaning and the shouting in my case all went to making me a centre half in the Premier League as a full-time footballer as opposed to a centre forward in the First Division as a part-timer.

There are many managers who, having bought me as a goal scorer, would have been so annoyed at me not making it in the position that they would have quit on me.

He didn't accept me for what I was supposed to be. He probed and worked to find if there was something else. He persevered and I am eternally grateful to him for that.

I have had and will continue to have – hopefully – a great career at what I always wanted to be, a professional footballer.

What if he had decided, 'This is a striker who isn't good enough,' and had let me go on my way?

How would I have reacted? What would my life have been? Would I have battled back or accepted, like so many do, that I wasn't good enough?

I like to think I would, like my brother, have gone on trying to prove I was good enough. But most of all I am glad I didn't have to find out any of these things because of Jim McLean.

The Boss is still built the same way, too.

In his first season with us, Jim McInally went from being an overweight young man with an uncertain run behind him with Celtic,

Dundee, Nottingham Forest and Coventry City to a Scotland player who will undoubtedly add to the couple of caps he has already won.

Our training really is special. I doubt if there is a fitter staff in the country than us – and it wasn't long before the extra weight dropped off young McInally.

We all took him to be a full back, but the Boss was looking deeper than that. He knew he could play there, but obviously didn't believe it was where he was best suited.

So what had happened to me happened to Jim – in reverse. Suddenly we found him alongside us in the first team against Hamilton Accies – in midfield. He has hardly missed a game since and his tackling and general play in front of me has been a delight to watch and played a large part in our (almost) very successful season 1986-87.

The only problem we at the back have with him is that blonde hair. His wife is a hairdresser and sometimes his 'highlights' really are dazzling.

Mind you, I once remember reading that one of the all-time greats of English football, Raich Carter, who was silver-haired, attributed a lot of the attention people paid to his ability to the fact that he was more easily noticeable than others who also had ability. So Jim's on a winner with the blonde thatch!

What you notice about another 'convert' isn't his hair, it's his build.

I'm talking about John Clark this time. He must be one of the most perfectly proportioned footballers of all time – a tremendous build allied to good balance and physical power in the air and with shooting which can be awesome.

He has played both centre forward and centre half though the Boss said in a recent interview that nothing had been decided in his mind about his eventual position.

Coming off the back against Barcelona he scored that wonderful headed goal. Then, when he moved up front against Gothenburg in the second game at Tannadice, he made an amazingly quick turn for his size and struck a great shot for our goal.

Hegarty, McInally, Clark . . . We are only three of the many players who have been moved around by Jim McLean and who have found or will find that, much though we thought we knew, we weren't really expert at reading what we are best at out there on the field.

For myself, I got a double boost with my move to central defence. I was in a position where I was comfortable at the very top level and was used in many dead-ball situations as a potential scorer, which satisfied the other side of my character and continued to realise my boyhood dreams of getting goals, of seeing that goal-net jump when I scored realised.

8
The Stein Lessons

Everyone noticed a change in manager Jim McLean in the season just past.

The media, in particular, were delighted. He was absolutely brilliant at Press conferences and, in return, got on better with reporters, cameramen and the rest than he has ever done.

There was a time when his relationship with the people who publicise the game wasn't all that hot. He seemed to be falling out with them regularly and they seemed to be 'knocking' him and the club equally regularly.

I am not an analyst, but I feel part of the reason at least for the 'new' image dates back to a spell as assistant to manager Jock Stein when the latter was Scotland boss.

Frankly I am first of all not surprised that Mr Stein chose our manager. I have said many times that I doubt if anyone in the game anywhere is better equipped in tactical knowledge and the ability to blend players into a unit.

In saying that I don't know how much of that sort of thing he did during his spell with Scotland, but if he wasn't used in this direction he should have been.

Back though to facts as opposed to theory.

I believe that, as a club manager, Jim McLean built an outstanding team – now he has actually built at least three – but always felt maybe his players weren't of the quality of the so called super-stars at other places.

Then he got the Scotland call and actually started to work with the best Scottish-born players in the game – and there aren't many better than them no matter which era you are considering.

They were there from Liverpool, Manchester United, you name it, every big club.

And I feel he realised, when close up, that the quality of his players at Tannadice was on a par in many cases with the best and, overall, inferior to none.

I recall him saying before the Scotland post that players at international level must be really good. On his return he reflected that Dundee United 'mustn't be a bad club at all.'

So that did his confidence a whole lot of good.

Then there was the Stein approach to the media. He knew how to handle himself with everyone on that side of the game, based on experience gathered in the great years with Celtic and on the broader canvas of international foootball.

Our Boss can give lessons – he can also take them – and I am sure he absorbed a whole lot of last season's 'new look' from his Stein experience.

He really is a fascinating character in many ways, and while people like me may moan at certain aspects of that character the sum total is that he is a superb manager who has proved himself again and again.

It isn't difficult to manage one great team, some take over one, some create one. The real secret in football management is to do it more than once and, even more difficult, do it with a club which isn't spilling over with riches, doesn't have tremendous crowds following them home and away.

We are like that at Dundee United. I am not in any way blaming anyone, but we do at times have gates which are a tenth of some of the giants of the game and, but for the shrewd buying and selling manoeuvres by the manager and the Board of Directors, of which he is now one, of course, there is little doubt United would have been among the also-rans of the game.

That is an honest opinion, not flattery. But I'll bet you this . . . I'll get stick for it from none other than Jim McLean.

I'll explain by giving you examples.

The club went on a pre-season tour of Germany in July '84. I left with mixed feelings as Linda was expecting our third baby and I knew the baby would be born while I was away.

Not that Linda wasn't being well looked after. She was with our next-door neighbours and very good friends Tom and Flo Farrell and their daughters Lynn, Jan and Audrey. Also Linda's parents, who took over when Christopher arrived.

During the tour we got the sad news that our chairman, Mr. Johnstone Grant, had died and, as club captain, I had to fly back for the funeral with the manager.

It was a sad occasion, but it did also mean I was able to see our new son, who had arrived two days after we left.

You know how it is at airports. Between flights or before them you have time on your hands. So what could be more natural than for

Paul Hegarty and Jim McLean to use that time talking about football – if we had talked about anything else it would have been a miracle!

Eventually, the chat got around to the time we beat Borussia 5–0 with one of the best displays I had ever seen from a United line-up.

I was talking about certain things that happened in the game, then went on to say that I thought he (the Boss) had been 'a bit out of order' in criticising certain players and making comments about our play on that occasion. I wondered out loud if it wouldn't have been better to have left well alone, the win had been so thorough and the overall performances so good.

That was when the insight into the man's honesty came through.

'Paul,' he said, 'that's the way I am. Things happened and I had to speak about them there and then.'

Others might have waited, let us savour the moment. To him it was a job well done, but there had been certain things not quite right so he had to get home his points as soon as we were available.

I also knew something else there and then. That I had got a bit too close to him for comfort and that he would make sure I knew that in the not-too-distant future.

Sure enough it came – on that very same tour which we both returned to after Mr Grant's funeral.

We were playing a Second Division team in the Black Forest after having beaten Cologne 2–1 and, in that game, having given an excellent performance.

There were only a few hundred spectators at the game with the Second Division club and it is fair to say we didn't exactly sparkle, even though we won.

But all through that game I could hear the voice of the manager from the touchline telling me what I was doing wrong, 'sorting me out' in no uncertain fashion.

He wants to speak to players, loves talking football, BUT HE NEVER WANTS TO GET TOO CLOSE TO ANY OF US BECAUSE OF WHAT HE MIGHT HAVE TO SAY OR WHAT HE MIGHT HAVE TO DO ONE DAY.

Can you imagine being a player with a manager who was always telling you how good you were, always giving you praise in public, then turning round and telling you you were being dropped?

The McLean way may seem harsh at times, but the end product of keeping distance between himself and players is something I would never criticise.

Another example of his approach came when Linda and I were

invited to a furniture show in Dundee.

We thought we were the only football folk invited, but, when we turned up, there was the manager with his wife Doris.

A manager's wife is an important part of a club, and I say here and now that Mrs McLean is a fine example.

Nights out at the theatre, get-togethers at various houses, she is there with the rest of the wives, no side, no difference, just one of the group.

After the show the boss and his wife invited us back to their house for a coffee. We spent a very pleasant hour.

On the Saturday, we played Hibs.

I didn't think I was all that bad – or all that good for that matter – but, as a defender, I rated no goals scored against us as success.

So what did I get when I came off at the end?

You've guessed it – a right old-fashioned going over. And, as the visitors' dressing room at Easter Road isn't all that well tucked away, the comments on my performance were overheard by several Hibs fans who no doubt deliberately make that part of their Saturday after-match ritual every home game.

One of them smiled as I passed him on the way to the bus afterwards. 'Don't worry son,' he said, 'I didn't think you were as bad as all that!'

Which only left me feeling worse seeing I didn't think I'd been bad at all.

But the bottom line is that, again the Boss was proving, apart from getting home a few lessons about my play, that he wasn't going to let me get too close.

He is the total, complete and utter professional. I can't say often enough that his magnificent record as a manager is deserved probably more than anyone else's I know of.

But I do wish he could unwind a bit. I can tell him as one of his longest-serving players ever that we would not think any less of him.

We know how he has guided and shaped successful careers for players over sixteen years. We know his methods are successful, but enjoying success with us would be a good thing all round.

I repeat that I am no analyst, but I believe he is happiest when he can be a tracksuit manager, when he can get involved in the actual game.

The day after European games, for instance, when we are usually allowed time off, he is at his desk at his usual time of just after 9 a.m., then really enjoys the next bit, when he can supervise the training with players who weren't in action the night before.

Then after a busy afternoon, he is, often as not, away at night watching a game at anything from schoolboy to international level.

It is a punishing schedule, but a proven success.

And how much he enjoys playing the game can be judged from last season's challenge matches between a team chosen by coach Gordon Wallace and himself and one from the media chosen by former East Fife 'keeper and now freelance journalist Dick Donnelly.

These games were played before our Europe ties, and though the totally biased Press men claim narrow defeats, the other side say it was at least 20–2 over three games.

To watch the boss and Gordon in those games proved beyond any possible shadow of doubt that actually playing is the greatest thing for a footballer, even when he leaves his top days behind him.

They loved every minute . . . not least when they stuck the ball in the net, which they both did a few times.

Looking on, it is rumoured that certain United players – no, a certain United player – actually criticised one or two aspects of the play of our top men.

Mind you, it was difficult to hear that criticism from more than a few yards' range, which is maybe a good thing for P–ul S–u–r–c– who, of course, I will not name.

Earlier in this chapter I was talking about events that happened in July '84, and in that same month I was really honoured to meet a hero of mine, Gary Player.

In a 'Player Profile' of myself in a programme one of the questions asked was 'Who would you most like to meet?' My reply – 'Gary Player'.

Richard Gough read this and said that if ever Gary was over here he would arrange for me to meet him, as he was a friend of Gary's son Wayne when he lived in South Africa.

True to his word, when Gary was here for the 1984 Open, Richard arranged for me to meet him – something I will always be grateful to him for doing.

Richard and I went to a house on the outskirts of Dundee where he was staying. I was really impressed with Gary and his attitude.

He was deep into psychology and believed it helped him to achieve many of his goals. A really interesting person.

9

Diego My Number One

Probably the most asked question of any footballer is, 'Who is the greatest player you have played against?'

Some may find that difficult. I don't. It has to be Diego Maradona – and not the Diego Maradona who took the football world by storm in the World Cup of 1986 in Mexico, but a stocky wee laddie who played for Argentina against Scotland at Hampden Park on June 2, 1979.

I happened to have the job of marking Leo Luque, who doubled up as striker alongside Mario Kempes.

He took me to areas of Hampden I didn't know existed. Had me thinking, 'what am I doing here?'

He would hang around looking as if all that interested him was the colourful scene on the terracing, or thoughts of home. Then the ball would be shoved forward and he would be off like a streak of light with me usually trailing in his wake desperately trying to get in a tackle.

I had played against some players who could shift over the ground at a fair rate of knots in my time, but never anyone with a burst of pace like this.

Now I'll anticipate your next question. Why am I talking about a bloke called Luque when I have said that the greatest player I have played against is Diego Maradona?

What I am doing is setting the scene, as they say in books and plays.

The Argentinians built their game from the back. If Scotland had done it the way they did, we would have been booed off the park.

Even as recently as the last game of the 1986-87 season, Scotland v. Brazil, I heard Scotland men getting stick because they tried to take the sting out of the Brazilians – who were absolutely brilliant, by the way – by knocking the ball around in front of our own penalty area.

What a Scottish crowd loves to see is a charge on the opposition goal. Don't we all! But try that against teams of the calibre of Brazil and Argentina and they'll kill you stone dead by what could be termed, in boxing language, counter-punching through the gaps you leave as you rush forward.

But back to that game in '79.

When the back lot decided the time was ripe to push the ball forward, they gave it to this stocky wee guy with jet black hair and legs like tree trunks, called Maradona.

All through my story I have emphasised that my greatest admiration is for players with little going for them in the way of height.

Here was another one. I had heard his name in our pre-match build-up, had noted that he was highly rated by the Boss, Jock Stein. But nothing had prepared any of us out there on the park for his all-round ability.

It didn't matter how the ball arrived, he had it under control instantly. And he wasn't stationary when he got it, he was in his stride and coming at us, drawing defenders, able to take them on on his own or pull them so out of position that one of his mates could get into an empty space in front of our goal.

He had a left foot like a magic wand, and just when I had decided there wasn't a right foot to go with it, he hit a 30-yard pass with his right which 'bent' and landed, as the old-timers say, with the lace pointing the right way, in front of Kempes . . . and I was off chasing again!

Do you remember the wonder goal Maradona scored against England in the World Cup of 1986? The one where he got to the ball in midfield and weaved past player after player before drawing Peter Shilton and gliding the ball past him?

I was watching on television and shouting that he was going to score long before he did, because I saw in that move all the great things he had promised at Hampden seven years earlier.

And I grieved for those England defenders as I grieved for myself at Hampden.

Then we had only one absolutely direct confrontation. He came straight at me with the ball at his feet. He was moving fast, the ball under perfect control.

I was stationary and as I moved forward to tackle he dipped his shoulder and started to go past.

There are instants in life frozen in your mind forever. This was one for me. I knew there was no way I could tackle him properly and expect to get the ball, I knew there was no way I could back off and 'run' him as I was already too committed.

So I did what any rugby man would do. I tackled him according to their code, waist-high, with a precision Ian 'Mighty Mouse' McLaughlan at his peak would have been proud of!

It stopped him all right – for a few seconds while I got the wrath of the referee's tongue.

Yes, Maradona is my No.1. He has control, pace, balance and vision. He can see three or four moves ahead, if not more, just like a great snooker player in a game that is played at many times the speed of the one on the green baize.

The Scotland team that night was Rough (with George Wood on as substitute); Burley, Munro, Narey, Hegarty, Hansen, McGarvey, Wark, Dalglish, Hartford (Frank Gray) and Graham.

We were beaten 3–1 with Arthur Graham getting our goal, which, allowing for the quality of the opposition, wasn't at all bad.

I don't like getting beaten, no footballer worth his salt does, but sometimes in a beating you have been privileged to be part of something else. We were privileged to be among the first to see the rise and rise of Diego Maradona in Europe.

Then there is George Best.

I choose Maradona because I played against him just before he reached his peak. With George Best I faced him at exactly the opposite end of his career – when he was deep into his 30's and playing for Hibs on a short contract.

I recalled, when I found out he was to face us, a game I had seen him in on television. It was Manchester United against Chelsea, and 'Chopper' Harris lived up to his name and tried to do just that to Best.

It seemed inevitable he would succeed, but with a change of pace and slight swerve the Irishman left the defender hitting thin air.

He then went on to chip the ball delicately over the head of Peter Bonetti, the Chelsea goalkeeper who later joined us for a short spell at Tannadice.

The Best I faced had lost the edge which made him such a legend in his own career, but there were times when he dipped a shoulder, or sent away a pass, or accelerated with that famous shuffle over a few yards when I found myself thinking, 'He must have been murder to play against at his peak'. Many who did play against him have told me since that he was.

And right up alongside those two true greats, I put another who must rate in the same class – Kenny Dalglish.

I played against him when he was beginning and as he developed, and I doubt if he was ever better than he was just before he left Celtic, even though the bigger stage in England may have made it appear different.

There are those who are quick to say that Dalglish was never a total success with Scotland, while at the same time giving him ten out of ten as a club player.

I, too, give him ten out of ten for his vision, bravery, hard work. He is a great shielder of the ball, making it almost impossible for defenders to get it from him without committing a foul, is reasonably good in the air, has an eye for goal and is a great all-round athlete.

And none of that disappears when he plays for Scotland.

Where he has fallen down – and surely this is a plus in a way – is that he works, or maybe it should be 'worked', so hard to be part of the team and to help others that his own game suffered.

If he had been able to become selfish when he pulled on a Scotland jersey, he would have been in the ten out of ten category at international as well as club football.

I am one of his admirers and feel I can speak with authority, having played with and against him.

Kevin Keegan didn't have the smooth skills of Maradona, Best or Dalglish. He was another of life's little guys who had to do battle to make it to the top, who had to work on his strengths so that he could gain the respect of his fellow professionals . . . and who succeeded beyond perhaps even his own wildest dreams as a young lad.

When I think on him I always have in my mind's eye another great striker, West German Uwe Seeler.

No, I didn't play against Seeler – I'm not THAT old! – but he was probably the first foreign-born striker I ever saw on television, and both he and Keegan were small and quick and great goal scorers.

I marked Keegan in a game against Southampton – and deserved every penny of my wages that week. He never stopped moving. He moved right, left, up the middle, back. Every run he made had the object of upsetting you, drawing you out of position. I didn't do badly against him but my main memory is of never having a second to relax in.

I must also comment on the sportsmanship of a player who could easily have let success in Britain and Europe go to his head.

I played against Keegan in a Scotland/England match at Wembley, a game I mention elsewhere. He scored and, at the end, I asked if he and I could swop jerseys as we had been direct opponents.

'I'm really sorry,' he said, 'Kenny [Dalglish] and I have a pact to swop jerseys. Tell you what, though, you'll get my jersey and I'll get yours next time we play against one another for our countries.'

Sadly, for me at any rate, we never did face up again.

So there you have it. Maradona the greatest, with Best, Keegan, Dalglish oh so close.

But they aren't the only ones in my top list.

Rudi Voeller of West Germany gave me a really hard time when he played against United for Werder Bremen. Again a player who never let up, with touches of both Keegan and Dalglish in his make-up.

And, at home, Derek Johnstone, in his heyday with Rangers, Mark McGhee when he was with Aberdeen, and Frank McGarvey with both Celtic and St Mirren.

Derek didn't do much running about – which is putting it mildly! But he was big and, unlike many big men, good in the air. I say unlike many big men because a lot of them seem to think if they are tall they don't need to jump . . . which suits me just fine.

He jumped, all right, and his timing was superb. Though he was a likeable big bloke, he dished out stick on the park, but, to be fair, took it as well.

Mark and Frank are awkward customers. I don't know often if even they know what they are going to do next, but it can be nasty for defenders whatever it is.

Then there is Alan Forsyth. Maybe some of you are saying, 'Who', so I'll explain. A couple of bad knee injuries cut short his career and it was marvellous he came back as he did with Raith Rovers. Now he was really hard, a really mean customer to play against as I discovered in practice games.

Had injuries not interrupted, I believe he would have gone right to the top.

His approach to the game was totally dedicated to winning – and the best example of that came in a Thursday morning practice game where our manager, Jim McLean, wanted to see the first team win to build them up for the Saturday.

'If you don't win you'll be back in the afternoon,' he warned. I was in the first team, Alan in the reserves and he really set about us. Result, a second-team win in the morning and a return in the afternoon.

'If you don't win you'll be back tonight,' said the Boss. Result, another second-team win inspired by Alan and a return at night.

Thank God we squeezed an odd-goal win at night or we would

have been playing in the wee sma' oors – and when the final whistle blew, the angriest man on that park was Alan, swearing that 'five more minutes and you'd have been back again'.

Finally, to a striker from the same city as I play in and, I hope, the end of a rumour which has grown into a story many people believe, but which is totally untrue.

I wasn't sorry when Eric Sinclair moved on to pastures new from Dens Park. He was a battler, a bustler, a striker who always gave defenders a hard time.

And many Dundee supporters believe I did him no good in a Cup tie which we eventually won 5–1.

They say I had him sent off – and nothing could be further from the truth.

He had elbowed me in the mouth early in the game and had a severe warning from the referee.

Then he did it again second half. It was a real belter which made me black out for a second or two and come round lying on the ground.

Yes, it was as bad as that. He DID catch me – and an elbow is as effective as a punch delivered by a professional boxer. I was really grounded, didn't, as some say, just fall down.

What I didn't know was that the linesman had spotted what was going on. HE drew the referee's attention to the incident. The REFEREE sent Sinclair off. All I had to do with it was getting in the way of his elbow – and that, believe me, I would have avoided if it had been at all possible.

I hope that clears up the misconceptions once and for all. I have met Eric on several social occasions since and we are on friendly terms.

10

That Narey Partnership

When I first moved to centre-half with Dundee United I teamed up at the back with Alex Rennie, later to be a highly successful manager with St Johnstone.

Alex was one of those players who only had to look at something fattening and he put on weight. After Christmas every year we have a weight check to see if we have been over-indulging.

Despite the fact Alex went around at the Christmas party held in his house saying, 'No thanks, that's fattening,' he always seemed to be in the sweat suit working off the extra pounds when he got back into training.

In the background briefly was a tall young lad from Dundee who was showing exceptional talent as a midfield player-defender. The betting at the time was that he would end up as an outstanding midfielder – but history dictated differently.

When everything settled down after the manager had worked away at the best line-up, Dave Narey was alongside me in the middle of the back four, an association which has now gone on for years and which I would be happy to continue for long enough.

I have been asked if we are 'psychic', we blend so well together. I remember Kevin Keegan and John Toshack being asked the same when they were with Liverpool and scoring goals every game.

There were even tests done with cards – checking to see if one knew what the other drew – to analyse their understanding. No one has done that with us; I don't think it is needed.

When you get together in a football team it takes time to realise you are a partnership. In my case I suddenly realised it had happened after about a couple of seasons. It felt right playing with Dave and we blended together.

The manager is a great one for blending in all departments. Look at the Paul Sturrock-Davie Dodds pairing we had for so long and which was such a success up front.

But back to Dave Narey. His nickname is 'Sash'. I know that is spelt wrongly, but that's the way we say it. It actually comes from what people thought was a striking similarity in looks to the French singer-guitarist-actor Sacha Distel. I explain who he is because younger readers might have forgotten him!

Nowadays others are inclined to say he looks more like Bob Geldof. All I am concerned with is that he is a great player.

We also room together – and thereby hangs a tale, or two.

He might not be the world's greatest sleeper, but he must be close. Given a chance, it's shut-eye time for him.

I remember rabbiting on one night about a game we had just finished – and suddenly stopping to ask his view on something. There was no reply. He was sound asleep . . . and had been almost from the time I started talking.

He also has the disturbing habit of sleeping with one eye open, not a pretty sight.

Actually the other players say I have to turn him over every hour or so just to make sure he is still with us, and that is right in the sense that no matter the commotion around in any hotel, or traffic noise from outside, big Dave can sleep through it and wonder next morning why everyone is fussing.

As players, we have different ingredients, which is probably one of the answers to why we seem to blend so well.

He is an excellent user of the ball, has great pace and his reading of the game is outstanding. He may not be, for his height – 6ft 1 ins – as good in the air as he might be, so maybe I sneak ahead on points on that one.

But the sum total of his talents is that he is an outstanding player who would be that in any company.

His consistency is legend – and also something which has a bit of a backlash at times. If he has a game which is even a fraction below his best there are people saying, 'Narey had a bad one today'. He has probably played better than anyone else in the team, but that doesn't count in their eyes.

I am mainly the centre-half, he is mainly in a sort of sweeper role, reading situations, intercepting danger and, when possible, moving up into midfield or further if that is 'on'.

We have played against some of the best in our ten years or so and I think we can safely say our record is excellent.

He is one of those people who is never flustered and is a genuinely nice person, but we don't socialise much outside the game and we seldom talk about it.

The understanding we have on the park is just something which is there and is also obviously something which manager Jim McLean spotted a long time ago – before even we realised it ourselves.

Only last season we met some of the best strikers in Europe playing for Borussia Munchengladbach, Barcelona and IFK Gothenburg.

Possibly the best known were Mark Hughes and Gary Lineker of Barcelona, who cost something like £5 million between them from Everton and Manchester United respectively, and against whom I played in the second leg of the quarter-final, having missed the first leg.

Because of our run in Europe and being the last British team involved, there was a lot of speculation about how we would cope with them, a lot of opinion that they would be a bit out of our league.

Dave and I knew of them, of course, but I can tell you now that we never really talked about them. They are in the position of making a lot of money for playing the game, of having huge transfer fees paid for them, so we reckoned the pressure was all on them.

The best player I have ever faced is Diego Maradona, but the Barcelona pair definitely come into the excellent category.

We gave them respect, but no more. After all, if you give someone too much respect you also give them an advantage. Our determination was that they wouldn't get the opportunity to show how good they were . . . and they didn't.

I recall Lineker saying to me over there, 'If you score we will fold.' How right he was.

We play a zonal marking system with the club, so I wasn't specifically looking after one or other. Both came into the areas I was responsible for at different times, but seldom caused me too much bother.

As well as not discussing much about games or individuals before a game, Dave and I don't talk too much on the park. The rapport we have can't really be explained, I'm just glad it is there.

In 15 years' time or so I might look back and say, 'We weren't bad players at all!' You can have one-season wonders, but it is the second, third, fourth, fifth, sixth and so on seasons of consistent play that really count, that can really be set against you in assessing your quality as a player. I believe we will pass the test.

One big regret I have is that Dave and I seldom got a chance of playing alongside one another at international level.

Both of us have been capped, of course, but seldom together as a central defensive pairing.

I have nothing against those I have been paired with – Gordon McQueen, Alan Hansen, Alex McLeish and so on. But why only once a Hegarty-Narey partnership?

I doubt it will happen now, but some day I must try and find out what was against us.

Did Scotland managers rate Dave more a midfield player than a central defender? Certainly there are those who say he moved back too quickly to defence at club level, that, as a midfield player, he could have been equally outstanding.

Was there always, bar that once against Northern Ireland, in the eyes of various Scotland bosses, someone better than one of us in a central defensive role?

I could go on asking questions like that, but the way I see it is that we were playing together season in season out, we were meeting and coping with the best not only in Scotland but also in Europe.

So why weren't we more often good enough as a pair for Scotland's central defensive job?

I remember hearing a discussion among some older fans some time ago. They were recalling a period when Rangers had the best defence in Scotland and Hibs the best forward line.

That defence was Brown; Young, Shaw; McColl, Woodburn, Cox. The forward line, Smith, Johnstone, Reilly, Turnbull and Ormond.

Yet they apparently never played as a team for Scotland. So maybe the fact that Dave and I didn't get the chance dates back to some theory that no matter how it looks, club football 'units' don't rate as good bets at international level.

I hardly need to emphasise that I most certainly don't agree!

I have gone on at length about Dave Narey because we have had such a tremendous partnership in the team for so long and I wanted to pay respect to his abilities.

But there have been many others who stand out in my memory as team-mates over the years. I choose them at random, so if you aren't mentioned don't think it is because I didn't respect your ability!

Frank Kopel – Nothing spectacular, but did his job as full back efficiently. Not fast, but covered this by his superb reading of the game. He wasn't a crowd favourite, but his mates appreciated him. Frank and his wife Amanda are great friends of Linda and me.

George Fleming – A grafter, a good players' player again. His greatest asset, apart from his ability to snap at people verbally and keep them on their toes, was that he was always available if you were in a tight situation.

Andy Rolland – The oldest teenager in the business. Remember Dick Emery and his ridiculous gear in his televised comedy shows? Andy was 33 when he'd come into training in all the gear – denim jacket, jeans and so on. As a player another excellent reader of the game. A character, but we can always do with some of them.

Jackie Copland – Stylish, very athletic, great build and stamina. Similar in many ways to Dave Narey. Quiet, unassuming and got on with the job effectively. He was also one of the great trainers.

Ian Macdonald – He came from Rangers and was one of the fastest movers I have ever seen with the ball at his feet. He gave defenders four, five, six yards and still beat them to get in great crosses.

Doug Houston – Now coaching part-time at Tannadice and teaching. Took me under his wing when I arrived. A really genuine person who is always there to help. When things were getting me down a bit early on at Tannadice he encouraged me to keep working at my game. As a player showed a great knowledge of the game from left midfield.

Archie Knox – Now assistant to Alex Ferguson with Manchester United and formerly Dundee manager. Always thought he could beat men, but wasn't really all that successful at it! Another great one for helping youngsters. Tremendous enthusiasm which rubs off on people around him.

Walter Smith – Now assistant manager of the 'new' Rangers who are having such sensational success. A thoughtful player and great reader of the game. It is absolutely no surprise to me that he has succeeded at Ibrox because he really is in the front rank of coaches. He can wield the big stick, but he also knows in training exactly to the split second when you have had enough. A great tactician who has an A to Z knowledge of the game.

Gordon Wallace – Now coach with us. A prolific scorer with a natural eye for a chance. Even today when he is playing in 'bounce' games you can see the talent for being in the right spot at the right time. He really brought on Paul Sturrock, showing him when to make runs, where to go, what to do. He was a great shielder of the ball, allowing Paul to move into position.

Maurice Malpas – Like Dave Narey he isn't always appreciated because his standard game after game is so high and people expect it of him. Great reader of the game, excellent user of the ball. I believe his best position is his Scotland one of full back, but after he plays a few games in midfield and settles in, I'm never too sure!

John Holt – Nothing showy, nothing flash, gets on with the job. An excellent professional who works tremendously hard in training and in games. An honest person and I'd always have him on my side.

Billy Kirkwood – A players' player who has had to live with people on the terracing criticising him when it shouldn't have happened. He is like George Fleming, always available when you are in a tight situation. He will take the abuse when you have put him in the mire and he has taken you out of it.

Eamonn Bannon – He can turn a game for you. What magnificent stamina! He is one of the engine room and what an engine he has himself! He doesn't look to have it but again and again he has proved he can go from our penalty area to the opposing bye line and back again in one move. The midfield in Scottish football is a place for players who never stop working. He is the best example of all.

Ralph Milne – A player who, on his day, is unbeatable. Like Eamonn can turn a game in an instant. I'll never forget when we beat Dundee 2-1 at Dens. Ralph was in the centre circle, looked up, saw the keeper off his line and chipped the ball into the net. An instinct player, frighteningly fast. It would be a full back's nightmare to face him and Ian Macdonald on the wings and on song at the same time.

Davie Dodds – Like Hegarty and Narey, he and Paul Sturrock worked well together. Davie took a lot of stick, Paul picked up the scraps. He really worked hard for us closing full backs down 18 to 20 yards out, making it awkward for them and stopping them getting forward, a clinical finisher who didn't usually score spectacular goals, but got them mostly from within the six yards box, but then any goal in your favour is a good goal. A very likeable person.

Paul Sturrock – He refers to himself as 'Little Bird' after the great Brazilian player of the 1950s. But if he knows so much about him is he THAT old?! Seriously, though ... when the ball is played up to him he has a great ability to turn defenders inside out. He has tremendous pace over 10-15 yards and is a great crosser of the ball. I will never forget that cross for Iain Ferguson to score against Barcelona. He strolled in and chipped the ball perfectly on to Iain's head.

Richard Gough – A great player, very single-minded about success. A winner. I think his best position is right back but time will tell. Great in the air and an exciting sight when he surges forward from the back.

Dave Bowman – Took a wee while to settle but is an important member of the side. Works really hard. A 'Just William' type, always at the capers, but that is good for team spirit.

Iain Ferguson – Another 'Just William' who was brought out of his shell with the European trips. Had some great seasons with Dundee and not such a good time with Rangers, but is now back on song. A clinical finisher. He does the business in his bit of the park and that is all you can ask for.

Jim McInally – Overweight when he arrived, but the level of training and standard of fitness here is second to none, so he was soon at his peak. Took about a couple of months to get into the side but has since gone from strength to strength. I am more than delighted that he has progressed to Scotland honours because he is a credit to the game. He is a first-class professional in every way with a tremendous work rate and loads of skill.

Kevin Gallacher – Sharp, good pace, an eye for goals. He has scored against all sorts of opposition and I believe that he will go on to be one of the best in a long, long time. Winger or main striker? A lot will depend on how he develops physically.

Ian Redford – Came from Rangers and maybe people thought he would be considering Tannadice second best. They don't know the man. He is a great professional and, in my view, will develop even further as a player. Has a magic left peg. Has a lot going for him off the park in the area of business interests, but that doesn't stop him being at all times completely dedicated to the game.

Dave Beaumont – A quiet man who gives it all when he is in the team. He is equally at home at the back or in midfield. An excellent member of the squad.

Gary McGinnis – He has done marvellously well to come back from his major ligament injuries, similar to those that have finished many a career. But his determination and application had to be seen to be believed.

John Clark – What a build, what power – and more skill with it than you usually find in someone so big. Remember the goal against Gothenburg? He turned on a sixpence and completely wrong-footed the defence. Then he bent in the shot, which proved his control of the ball is on a par with his ability to hit it so hard I wouldn't want to be in the way. Centre-half or centre-forward? Again time will tell.

And in case you are wondering . . . I haven't missed out Billy Thomson. He is in a separate chapter along with Hamish McAlpine!

11

Panic When Hamish Missed

Apart from brief spells in between, I have only really played in front of two goalkeepers with Dundee United and three at full international level.

With United it has been the one and only Hamish McAlpine and his successor, Billy Thomson, who joined us from St. Mirren in the summer of 1984 for a reported £70,000.

With Scotland, Alan Rough, the most capped 'keeper ever at international level in Scotland; George Wood, when he was with Everton; and Billy Thomson again, who was in the team in what is (to date!) my last international, a 0-0 draw with Northern Ireland in Glasgow in May, 1983.

Hamish is a one-off, a character, a person who has that special something about him that endears him to the crowd.

It wasn't always so. When he was in his earlier days, his style wasn't of the kind people were used to with 'keepers. They were constantly talking about mistakes or possible mistakes, often missing the outstanding things about his play, which was, admittedly, different from the average as far as goalkeeping was concerned.

He is a natural born athlete. There is a theory that he could have been a top-class professional golfer if he had decided to hit the wee ball instead of stopping the big one. I wouldn't argue with that, having been close up to his ability on the course often enough.

Having said that, I believe his real ambition was to be a great outfield player.

He was his own man, did his own thing – and one of them was that he had no special routine in training. I often think when I read of the punishing performance such as Peter Shilton puts himself through to remain at the top that you should never be too dogmatic about preparation in football. Every man is different, every one – within reason – has the perfect method of making him play at his peak.

Hamish's favourite training method was to play outside left in practice games!

And even here it wasn't a normal outside left's performance.

Nothing gave him more pleasure than taking the ball in his stride, moving a few yards and pinging it 60-65 yards in a pass to the man on his side furthest away in an attacking position.

Whether the move was 'on' or not, the sheer joy he got from hitting the ball that distance and finding a man was worth admission money on its own.

He was a great striker of the ball, perfectly balanced, hitting it exactly right. So right, in fact, that he went through a spell where he was even taking our penalties.

It was one of those times when we ran out of penalty takers. Yours truly was among the failures with a few misses. When the taking of penalties was mentioned everyone seemed to have something else to do.

The thing looked like developing into a crisis situation until Hamish broke in with his favourite phrase – 'No problem lads' – and volunteered to take them.

Now I can reveal exclusively our plan in case he missed! And he did miss a few as well as scoring.

The idea was that if the opposing 'keeper saved his kick we would rush into the box and try and obstruct him, stop him from throwing or kicking the ball upfield so that his team-mates had a chance of a go at a 'keeperless' goal.

At the same time, Hamish was to set off on his 100 yards or so dash back to his charge. He never was the best sprinter in the world, so it meant the 'obstructors' had a busy time on their hands with the opposing 'keeper, delaying his kick as long as possible.

I'll never forget an incident at Ibrox of all places when Peter McCloy did actually save one of Hamish's kicks.

He set off back towards our goal, we piled in on Peter, being careful not to foul him, only prevent him from clearing the ball. It seemed like half-an-hour passed as we messed about and, out of the corner of my eye, I could see that Hamish wasn't yet back where he should have been.

Suddenly, Peter escaped our 'trap' and hoisted a great ball forward. As I watched it drop perfectly for several Rangers players I thought 'that's it . . . a goal.'

But Hamish put everything into those last few yards and, from the middle of an almighty scramble in our goalmouth, he emerged with the ball in his hand waving everyone forward as if the whole situation had been no bother at all to him.

A 'keeper who played sweeper as well was not in the coaching manuals or within the orbit of most people who watched the game at that time.

But that is what Hamish was – a 'keeper-sweeper. He didn't hesitate to come out and tackle forwards, or head away the ball. And he loved it when he won a bit of room and was able to let go one of his 65 yard passes to one of our front men.

He was deadly accurate with throws from hand or kicks from hand. We had many an attack start directly from a shot at him which he fielded, instantly firing the ball back upfield right to someone like Paul Sturrock's feet deep in the opposing half.

I have been asked how we as defenders coped with this unusual style of goalkeeping, how we knew when he was staying in or coming out of goal.

The answer is that we found it easy because we knew the man and his style.

I can best illustrate that with an example from a game which some say was one of my best ever – against Werder Bremen in the second leg of the UEFA Cup, fourth round, in Bremen on December 6, 1982. We had won the first leg 2-1 in a tense game at Tannadice two weeks earlier.

I scored a goal that night from a set piece, but that wasn't the really vital moment in the game.

That came when Rudi Voeller, the German internationalist and an outstanding player who caused us plenty of worrying moments, tried a chip shot.

Now, to set the scene, you have to appreciate that he and his team-mates had spent a night of almost total frustration. We were holding on to a 2-1 lead, but only just. They had struck the ball against bodies, legs, heads, posts, crossbar and it simply would not go in.

But, this time, Hamish had come off his line and the whole German team and their massed ranks of supporters must have been ready to take off as Voeller's cleverly flighted shot rose above and out of reach of our 'keeper and began to drop into the empty goal.

What they didn't appreciate was that, because of the way play had been set up, I knew instinctively that Hamish was on his way out of his goal.

So I didn't waste time looking to check, just turned and hared back to the goal-line. I was there an instant before the ball and hooked it well clear.

In their frustration, the Germans were screaming that the ball had gone over, that it was a goal – and I'll bet there were a few hearts in mouths among the United supporters.

But I can assure you without any shadow of doubt that it was not. That I cleared it before it went over the line. Moments later, when all the fuss had died down, I knew for sure that we had won the game and were on our way into the next round.

Yes, Hamish looked unpredictable, but he wasn't and I feel we had a great understanding between him and the other defenders.

Off the field, he wasn't one to get too involved in football discussion – probably because he always seemed too busy in other directions. You could depend on him, he was a bit of a father figure in his way and when people wanted him to help with charities, in opening fêtes or such like, he was always there. Then, of course, there was his golf . . .

Now he has a public house in Dundee and with his cheery, outgoing attitude you can bet he will be a success.

Like everyone in the game, though, Hamish's career had to end some time. With us (he went on to Raith Rovers, of course) that came two or three seasons ago.

By this time, Billy Thomson was with us and, frankly, didn't have too good a start.

For this, the defenders in front of him must definitely take a share of the blame.

Let's recap. Behind us for years we had Hamish. We knew his style, we knew (just about) his every move as I illustrated with the Werder Bremen incident.

Then suddenly, first of all because of injury to Hamish, there was a new man behind us.

We should have appreciated immediately that he needed help, that we had to study him as much as he had to study us, and work together as a unit.

It just didn't happen at first. Used to Hamish and the way he was with them, conducting a choir behind his goal, always liable to pull off the impossible save or give them a heart-stopping moment, the crowd didn't take kindly to the big newcomer.

They even contrasted in looks. Hamish maybe a bit small for a 'keeper and dark, Billy 6ft 2ins and fair.

It was an uneasy spell, mostly for Billy. I have since told him that we appreciate we didn't help him enough at first. Typically he shrugged off the idea.

He had to go back into the reserves when Hamish returned and everyone in the club was impressed by the way he buckled down to his job, worked harder and harder to show how good he was.

And we knew he WAS good. We had played against him many times when he was with St. Mirren and reckoned he must have carried a rabbit's foot in his pocket – the saves he brought off to frustrate us again and again.

You don't lose the kind of ability he had – but we didn't appreciate how difficult it was to follow someone who was a legend and a 'different' 'keeper.

Then Hamish went out again and Billy came back, this time having been at the club long enough to get used to our ways and to have us understand his style of goalkeeping.

Since then it has been almost uninterrupted progress for the big man. Some of his saves have bordered on the incredible: flinging himself across goal to fingertip away shots I would have sworn he had no chance of reaching, tipping over 'certainties' to go in.

Hamish was a great reflex 'keeper with on-the-line saves, Billy is great to have coming for corner kicks and cross balls, which because of his height and timing he can get to before they become dangerous.

He also, as I have said, isn't missing when it comes to the goal-line saves either.

And what about his bravery?

It is as impressive as that Hamish showed on many occasions. And I need go back no further than the game in Gothenburg, the first leg of the UEFA Cup final last season, for proof of that.

When he went down at the feet of Lennart Nilsson I thought at first that it was a brave save. I didn't realise how brave until moments later when I got closer and saw blood everywhere.

What happened was that Billy's ear had been caught by a boot. I am not exaggerating when I say the ear was almost torn off.

If he had had to go off the field for repairs, no one would have uttered a word of criticism, but he was treated and bandaged by physiotherapist Jim Joyce and carried on playing.

Stitches were put in the terrible wound by club doctor Harry Leadbitter at half-time, when Billy admitted his head was 'ringing a bit' and he went out and brought off some more marvellous saves in the second half.

He has his own dry sense of humour, too. When the Press asked him how it had felt getting the stitches out later, his reply was, 'Not bad . . . except that I had my hand ready in case the ear fell off. That's one thing I wouldn't have dropped.'

12

Euro Start Extraordinary

I was reading through a list of United's European appearances the other day, and not only is it like a travelogue of the Continent, it is also a condensed version of the success of the club over the past couple of decades.

I have been told many times since – don't forget I wasn't even in my teens at the time – that even the most optimistic United supporter didn't expect anything other than defeat in the very first excursion into Europe in 1966.

Not surprising really when you consider they were drawn against Barcelona, then, as now, one of the world's major clubs.

But, like us 21 years on, they won – not just at home, but in the magnificent Nou Camp Stadium as well.

It was 2-0 for United at Tannadice, 2-1 over there.

And the team that set the club off on a European trail which has, so far, seen the appearances tally reach 80 was the same as for the second leg.

On both occasions it was Davie, Millar, Briggs, Neilson, Smith, Wing, Seeman, Hainey, Mitchell, Gillespie, Persson.

In the next round they met a club equally as big as Barcelona – Juventus – but even though they won 1-0 at home, they couldn't overcome the 3-0 defeat in the first leg in Italy.

Still directly connected with the club, then as a player, now as a director, is centre half Doug Smith. He actually went on to play 15 games for United in Europe and I doubt if any other club has on its Board of Directors a person with a record like that.

The thing that impresses you about the teams United have had representing the club in Europe is the continuity that runs through the list of names.

For instance, there is the goalkeeping situation.

In that first game and for four others, it was Sandy Davie. Then Donald Mackay had a five-game run before Hamish McAlpine was chosen.

He racked up an astonishing record.

Eight European Cup ties, four European Cup Winners Cup ties

and 39 UEFA encounters. It was almost an unbroken run, too, stretching from 1970 through to 1985, but Billy Thomson slipped in once against AIK Stockholm, away, in September, 1984.

Hamish actually played in our first UEFA Cup in 1985-86, against Bohemians away, but lost out to Billy for the return.

Now his tally of European ties with us stands at 17, to add to the six from his St Mirren days. Four goalkeepers used over 21 years and 80 games in Europe must be some sort of a record, especially with two of them having some 70 between them.

The name Narey keeps appearing on team sheet after team sheet, too. His debut was against Juil Petrosanki back in September, 1974 when he was 18 – and he set off on what is now a 63 games record with a goal.

The team when he made his debut was – McAlpine, Rolland, Kopel, Copland, Smith, Narey, Houston, Gardner, Gray, Fleming, McDonald.

He was in for three of the four games that season, but was a substitute for the fourth, which United lost 1-0 away to Borsapor. He scored one of his six 'Euro goals' on his debut.

This was European Cup Winners Cup year, by the way. We have never won the Scottish Cup, no matter how near we have come on occasions, but in season 1973-74 Celtic beat us 3-0 in the final and we got into the Cup Winners Cup because they had already qualified for the European Cup itself by winning the league title.

Another name which edged into the frame that season was Paul Sturrock. He got on as a substitute against Petrosani in the first game.

His style, as it developed, was made for playing against the Continental sides. Time and again when we go away you find the opposition asking how he is playing, is he scoring many goals?

Actually he hasn't scored that many in Europe – nine to be exact in 56 outings, but if assists were credited he would probably top the list.

One of the great moments in Europe as far as I am concerned came against Barcelona when he strolled in from the left and lifted the ball onto Iain Ferguson's head for him to score.

My European debut came in September, 1975, against Keflavik of Iceland.

The team was – McAlpine, Rolland, Kopel, Copland, Houston, Narey, Rennie, Payne, Hegarty, Fleming, Gray. Dave Narey had both our goals in the first leg and I had one of our four in the return at

Tannadice, when Addison, Hall and Sturrock took over from Copland, Fleming and Gray.

It wasn't until almost exactly two years later, though, that the Hegarty-Narey pairing went on the team list in that order.

Over those two years there had been the moves which ended with me in the position I have held for such a long time now, centre-half.

Dave was still to play in some games as a midfield man, but mostly we were paired at the centre of the defence.

That first game was against K.B. Copenhagen. The team was McAlpine, Rennie, Kopel, Robinson, Hegarty, Narey, Sturrock, Wallace, Kirkwood, Addison, Payne.

We won 1-0 with Sturrock getting the goal.

We were in for a rude awakening second leg, though. We lost 3-0 away and went out of the UEFA Cup in the first round.

It had happened once before, in 1969 when Newcastle United won 2-1 at Tannadice and 1-0 on their own St James's Park, and was to happen once again, the very season after Copenhagen when Standard Liège beat us 1-0 away and we could only draw 0-0 at home.

It is a depressing feeling going out that early in Europe, but the record isn't at all a bad one for a club so often involved. Three times in all those seasons – and not since 1978 . . . no, not bad at all.

The team for that second leg was McAlpine, Rolland, Kopel, Robinson, Hegarty, Narey, Sturrock, Wallace, W. Smith, Addison and Payne – only one change, Wattie Smith for Kirkwood – from the first game.

That Hegarty-Narey partnership remained the same over the next 50 consecutive games in Europe – with one exception. When Derek Stark took over for the injured Dave against Hamrun Spartans in the second leg of our European Cup tie in September, 1983.

The 'partnership' therefore went from 1977 to the first leg against Lens in the 1986-87 campaign which was to prove oh so nearly successful for us, with that one-game exception.

Definitely a record to be proud of.

But possibly the major factor in our relative success in Europe has been continuity in all sorts of positions.

Look at Eamonn Bannon. He had a 34 consecutive games run in his total of 48 European ties since joining us from Chelsea for a club record fee of £165,000 in October, 1979.

Maurice Malpas is still only 25, yet he has played 35 games in Europe since his debut in December, 1981 against Winterslag.

And what of unsung heroes like Billy Kirkwood?

He made his debut against K.B. Copenhagen the night the Hegarty-Narey partnership was first given the numbers 5 and 6. Although he moved on to Hibs briefly and returned to us only last season, he has so far had 40 European appearances.

John Holt is another invaluable member of the squad and has 33 European appearances behind him, while newcomers like John Clark, who got three of our 14 goals in the UEFA Cup last season, and Jim McInally are already on the 10 mark in European games played.

Then there are our ex-Rangers, Ian Redford and Iain Ferguson. Redford played 10 times in Europe with Rangers and scored one goal before coming to Tannadice.

With us he now has a tally of 15 games in which he has scored an astonishing seven goals. Not bad for a midfield man . . . and very probably part of the reason he got into the Scotland squad last season.

Iain Ferguson's games in Europe total seven and in them he has netted four goals.

He didn't appear in our colours until the quarter final ties against Barcelona last season because he was signed after the deadline. Then he missed the first leg of the final against Gothenburg because of suspension following two yellow cards.

His four goals show the quality of the player, though. They have been scored against Inter-Milan, Barcelona and Borussia. If there was a Super League in Europe, they would all be in it!

In a defensive role I manage to head clear as Dundee's George McGeachie tries to connect with the ball.

Disappearing fast into the distance, that's me smack in the centre of the pic, after scoring in our 5-0 defeat of Winterslag.

Another incident against Winterslag. I'm up for the ball but beaten to it by the keeper.

Hamish McAlpine and I showing we had played 50 consecutive games as 'keeper and centre-half one season.

In a tackle while playing Wales, with Kenny Dalglish in the background.

St Anthony's school team – from left (back) – Mike Devlin, Gavin Hancock, Mark Williamson, Gordon Knowles, Alex Wright, Joe Phair, Alex McNulty; front – John McMullan, Steve Hancock, Jim Love (captain), Paul Hegarty, Gerry Bannon, who is, incidentally, brother of my long-time United team-mate Eamonn Bannon.

Battling it out with Sandy Clark when he was with Rangers – with Dave Narey wondering where we have gone.

A proud moment as I wear a Scotland jersey.

Another of the great moments in Europe – scoring against Borussia Munchengladbach.

The fans look on as I show them the League Cup after a presentation at Dundee's City Chambers.

Back from that wonderful win in Barcelona last season. Linda and the family – from left – Paul, Mark and Christopher.

13

Games That Made History

Europe is a different ball game to domestic football.

It has been known for teams to find themselves in a hotel in a part of town where the traffic noise goes on all night – and all the party's rooms looking out on to the main road.

There's nothing worse than a bad night's sleep before a vital game – although, as I mention elsewhere, Dave Narey would never notice traffic or anything else. But then he is almost a one-off in the sleeping stakes.

Then there is a search for a training ground – and not much help being given to find one for the visiting club; a shortage of footballs for match practice . . .

I could go on, but you get the picture. In a European Cup tie you have to be prepared to ignore the little upsets calculated to make you edgy and get on with the preparation and the game itself.

Before I joined United I had been on one trip abroad – to Cyprus with Hamilton Accies. We played in a competition involving ourselves, Stoke City and Sheffield United.

I thoroughly enjoyed the experience and still do enjoy travelling to places I have never been before.

In the Stoke team – this was back in 1974 – there were legendary figures in the game like Gordon Banks and Geoff Hurst.

Banks and Hurst were in the England team which won the World Cup in 1966 and Banks is the 'keeper who brought off what the one and only Pele describes as the greatest-ever save in the World Cup of 1970.

That was when Pele got up to a ball a few yards out and headed it down for goal.

No normal 'keeper would have got to the ball, but Banks not only did that, he also managed to flick it so that it went over for a corner.

Hurst, of course, was the first man to score a hat-trick in a World Cup final, the 1966 one where England met West Germany at Wembley.

He was a tall, athletic player whose height and weight helped him hold the ball against heavy tackling.

There was also Alan Hudson. How he managed only a couple of caps for England must be down to his individuality, not his ability. We pride ourselves that we produce ball players in Scotland, but he could do all the ball control things AND pass accurately 30-40 yards.

If he had been playing now I doubt if any country could have chosen not to play him.

In the Sheffield United side were Scots Jim Brown and Eddie Colquhoun and another player I am still surprised didn't get any England honours, Alan Woodward.

He was silver-haired but younger than that indicated, and his pace, crossing ability and shooting power made him as good as any I have ever seen playing off the right wing.

I know my acquaintance with these people was brief, but there is no doubt in my mind that both Hudson and Woodward came into the category marked 'special,' every bit as much as Banks and Hurst did.

But then I don't pick teams – not yet at any rate!

I have gone on about this trip because it was my first experience of being, as it were, a full-time footballer in the sense that our team was together for ten days with no jobs outside the game to worry about.

On trips like this you find out about your team-mates, they find out about you. It's great for team spirits when, normally, you only meet for evening training or on match days.

And when you also start to mingle with players who have done and seen the lot it's a bonus.

The Cyprus break went all too quickly...in one respect. In another, I'm glad we left when we did because, within days, the Cyprus war broke out. That I can do without, thank you!

A year after this I had joined Dundee United and was going abroad on serious business.

This was to play Icelanders Keflavik in the UEFA Cup. My first 'proper' game outwith Scotland – and I wondered what we were in for when I saw the Iceland landscape. Talk about bleak! It looked like all rocks and boulders, with the brightly coloured houses happily breaking the monotony.

The people were great, though, and, as we won 2-0 through two Narey goals, it was a wonderful start to Europe as far as I was concerned.

Keflavik weren't and aren't in the top flight of European teams, but their enthusiasm is tremendous and here and there they have good players.

What I learned right away, even though they weren't a Juventus or Real Madrid, was that this was a different type of game to what we played at home.

It was more thoughtful with less hustle and bustle. That made it less demanding physically, but more demanding mentally.

Whereas at home things happen at what seems 100 miles an hour sometimes, the Europeans are slow to build things up, though anything but to finish them off.

So you have to be watching every move they make. If you lose out on a man who slips into a dangerous position you are in trouble, because rest assured the man with the ball will find him.

Since Keflavik, the years and the games have rolled on, sometimes, it seems, rolled into one.

We have got so used to playing in Europe with United that, on the few occasions when we have gone out of whatever competition we were involved in in the early stages, there has been a 'lost' feeling.

Not that there isn't plenty to play for back home. If you do go out early there might still be the League Cup, Scottish Cup and league – all three major home events. Even if you are out a wee bit later, there are still the Scottish Cup and league championship.

But Europe is the icing on the cake, different, special.

I love every minute of every game in whatever European tournament we are in, but there are obviously games which stand out in my memory as extra-special.

The standard is so high overall, they do not amount to many - six to be exact, with two of them against Borussia Munchengladbach and including that one against Keflavik because it was my first.

And two of them came in the same season, 1981-82, one in the first round against ASC Monaco, the other in the second round against Borussia.

First it was Monaco.

In football you plan to score goals, but seldom on the day, or night, does it all come together and get you the goals you want.

The night of September 16, 1981, though, it all happened for us on the scoring front. We got five goals, our equal second top tally to the seven we scored against Slask Wroclaw a year earlier.

Two of them came from the penalty spot and were netted by Eamonn Bannon, two came from Davie Dodds and one from Billy Kirkwood.

That night, we could do nothing wrong. The moves flowed like they were supposed to, we had people popping up everywhere seeking goals.

And don't get the impression that they were a bad side. In fact they were a very good side indeed, scoring two against us over there and beating us 2-1 at Tannadice. A final tally of 6-4 shows that they were good, but, on the night over there we were even better.

You feel it when things are going right. You hit the ball properly, there are always alternatives when you go to create a move, the shouts are right, the atmosphere is right.

That was how it was in Monaco.

But that isn't all I remember it for. We were staying in possibly the finest hotel we have ever stayed in - and that is saying something. It had its own private beach and all-in-all I kept being reminded of the scene in that television series 'Fantasy Island'.

When we are having one of those bad winters at home with snow and ice everywhere and seemingly everyone suffering from colds and flu, I often think back to that trip.

It was very warm, but not too warm, the hotel and surroundings were magnificent and the people marvellous and we capped it all by giving one of the greatest performances ever as a team.

There was a raft moored about 50 yards out to sea and every spare minute they had, the strong swimmers, like John Holt, got out on it to sunbathe.

And though the hotel was a plushy place by any standards the guests were great.

We had our own table for our meals and some of the lads wound up Hamish McAlpine to throw Billy Kirkwood into the swimming pool after dinner one night.

It duly happened, and it wasn't the players who enjoyed it most, it was the other guests.

In the very next round we were drawn against Borussia Munchengladbach, rightly rated one of the outstanding teams on the Continent, never mind their own country of Germany.

The first leg was away in their Bokelberg Stadium, an imposing sort of ground which looms all round you.

They beat us 2-0 and probably deserved to, though we weren't doing at all badly until the roof fell in with them netting their goals.

It might actually be that this was their undoing. If they had come over with a poorer result they might have been better off.

What actually happened was that they came to Scotland believing the tie was all over, that they would quietly humble this 'country cousins' team.

By this time, though, we had been around in Europe for a few years, we weren't easily overawed and had learned no game is over at what is effectively half-time in a European tie.

The second leg was on November 3, 1981, at Tannadice and we gave a nearly full house more than their money's worth.

It was similar to the Monaco experience, only this time at home instead of away. We moved perfectly as a team and, again, scored five goals, well deserved and well executed.

When your feelings are that your performance matched the score-line, then you have played the perfect game. These were my feelings that night. We have played as well, probably, but never better.

The Germans were obviously thinking they had the game sewn up and, when we hadn't scored after nearly half-an-hour, it seemed to confirm their opinion.

Then Ralph Milne struck with a typical goal. The timing was perfect because if it had been delayed any longer, the crowd might have started getting on our backs a bit.

Instead, they were willing us on, they sensed something special was in store – and it was.

Billy Kirkwood got a second just before half-time and the arrogance of the Germans had totally disappeared as we went off for a half-time talk which mostly consisted of the manager telling us to keep the momentum going.

The Germans rallied briefly at the start of the second half, but were soon shell-shocked by a third goal, this time from Paul Sturrock, who had been tormenting them all night.

I am proud of all the goals I have scored, but prouder of none than the fourth one that night. All right, I only had to side foot it in from a few inches, my favourite distance (!), but when folk look up the records of one of the club's greatest-ever nights they'll see my name on the score sheet.

That said, the real 'high' came with the fifth goal. I don't know where Eammon Bannon gets all his energy from out there on the park, but this goal showed how much is there.

He got the ball out to the left, then as he got nearer their goal started cutting in. There was one defender left between him and their goal and he sidestepped him in full flight and crashed the ball into the net.

It was a goal of stunning brilliance and totally demoralised the Germans – not just Borussia suffered, the shock waves went right through German football.

I'm told that in the 1950s the Hungarians came to Britain and showed Scotland and England how far we had fallen behind in the game. Our performance that night had the German football establishment thinking along the same lines about their game.

14

Most Capped Linesman?

I believe I am unique in international football. Put another way – do you know of any other linesman who has been capped by his country?

It happened in Canada in 1983. I was there as a member of the Scotland 'pool' which played three games against the host country.

In one practice match we were playing against a University side. I was on the bench when Jock Stein turned to me . . .

I had played against Northern Ireland in the home international in the season just ended but had missed out on the Wales and England games, so my immediate thoughts were, 'He's going to put me on.' And that could have been the start of another run of caps.

But what Mr Stein actually said, was, 'Hey, Paul, going to run the line for me?'

So I did and may well qualify either as the only linesman to play for his country, or the most-capped linesman in history.

Actually I have been capped eight times at full international level and twice as an over-age Under-21 player.

The first honours came in the home international series at the end of season 1978-79. You never actually know you are going to be honoured, but in my case Press speculation had been growing and our manager, who knows the game from A to Z, was going a bit further and saying 'you have a good chance.'

I tried as best I could to just go on playing and concentrating on each club game as it came, but I couldn't help feeling excited. After all, that wee lad playing on the drying green in Edinburgh had always imagined he was doing it in a Scotland jersey, and to represent your country in any walk of life is a tremendous honour.

Yet it was still a shock when the official letter stating 'you are in the pool for the home internationals against Wales, England and Northern Ireland . . .' actually arrived.

Without any shadow of doubt it was one of the proudest moments of my life. I must have read over the letter a dozen times.

Having said that, I assessed the situation as being that I had been included in the pool for experience. That I wouldn't play but would be involved in the build-up to the three games.

When we got together I was meeting big-name players like Graeme Souness and Kenny Dalglish, both then at their peak, for the first time close up.

It would be easy to be overawed, but, while I respected them, I took the view that, having been chosen for the pool of players, I was as good as anyone in my position in the game, so we were level pegging.

Self-belief stopping short of over-confidence is one of the vital factors in a footballer's make-up. People like Souness and Dalglish certainly have that. I concentrated on my own self-belief and on working hard as we built up towards the first game – against Wales at Cardiff.

Manager Stein wasn't involved in the direct training, but he was always there with comments, words of advice, watching how you coped with situations in the practice sessions, watching how much you put into training, how sharp you were.

On the last training session the day before the game he called me over and said simply, 'You are in the team tomorrow.'

Talk about not knowing what to think! I had, as I say, reckoned I was in for experience . . . yet here I was actually going to play.

Immediately on our return to the team's hotel I phoned Linda. There must have been some quick planning at her end because, at Ninian Park next day, she was there along with my father, her father and my brother Kevin sitting in the stand. They made a round trip of roughly 1000 miles.

The two teams that day were: Wales – Davies; Stevenson, J. Jones, Phillips, Dwyer, Mahoney, Yorath, Flynn, R. James, Toshack, Curtis.

Scotland – Rough; Burley, F. Gray, Wark, Hegarty, Hansen, Dalglish, Hartford, Wallace, Souness, Graham.

They substituted Nicholas for Yorath, and Jordan came on for us with Wallace going off.

Now, the perfect ending to this story would be of a magnificent victory by a Scotland team playing perfect football . . . and me scoring the winner in the last minute.

Which is the stuff dreams are made of – and dreams don't come true all that often. That one certainly didn't.

Wales won 3-0 – every goal scored by John Toshack.

I talked in the earlier part of the book about smaller blokes like myself working harder because we had more to prove than lads of average or above-average build.

Here was a player of above-average build who had worked hard at his game and had an eye for a chance second to none. His partnership with Kevin Keegan at Liverpool was the talk of football, but in this game he proved he didn't need any particular player alongside him to show how good he was.

It wasn't that we missed much in the air or on the ground in the central defensive positions, but big Tosh was at his absolute deadliest when anything did escape our attention.

The atmosphere was terrific and he responded perfectly with that hat-trick. Much as it was his 'birthday' as far as converting chances went, it was the opposite at the other end. We created them, but couldn't put them away, which is a fault that has been noticeable in Scotland teams for a long time.

After a brief return to our headquarters at Porthcawl a pretty subdued Scottish party returned to Glasgow to prepare for the midweek game against Northern Ireland at Hampden.

There was no great public criticism by the manager of the performance against Wales, but possibly his team changes told most about how he saw it.

Though there was a shuffling around of numbers – I for instance became a No 10 instead of a No 5, Graeme Souness a No 6 instead of a No 10 – I stayed centre-half, with a new partner beside me, a new goalkeeper behind me and a new striker in front.

They were George Wood in goal for Alan Rough, Gordon McQueen in central defence in place of Alan Hansen and Joe Jordan moving off the substitute's bench to start in place of Ian Wallace.

The teams which lined up at Hampden on May 22, 1979 were: Scotland – Wood; Burley, F. Gray, Wark, McQueen, Souness, Dalglish, Hartford, Jordan, Hegarty, Graham.

Northern Ireland – Jennings; Rice, Nelson, J. Nicholl, Hunter, Moreland, B. Hamilton, McIlroy, Armstrong, Sloan, Spence.

Dave Narey and Frank McGarvey came on for Wark and Graham and their sub was Scott for McIlroy.

Though, as I have said before, I would have liked to have played with Narey alongside me in the back four, I enjoyed having Gordon McQueen as my partner.

He was a 'big-timer', too, with Leeds United and Manchester United, but you wouldn't have known it. Last year I was at a coaching course in Largs and met him when he arrived there with his family on a day out.

We had a great chat and I am delighted he is back in the game as Airdrie manager. I wish him well – except, of course, when they meet us!

The performance this time wasn't five star, but it was better. We won 1-0 through a Graham goal. But what I remember most about the game was my first competitive sight of that truly remarkable goalkeeper, Pat Jennings.

He was so cool, so much in command. It was no surprise to me that he kept going until he was 40. When it was needed he could move fast all right, but his positioning and timing were such that most of the time he made everything look simple. That is the mark of a great goalkeeper . . . a great player, in any position, too.

So, with one win and one defeat under our belts it was off to meet England at Wembley.

I don't care what anyone says about other games, this one is special for any Scot. You could feel it from the moment we arrived at St Albans for our pre-match get-together, and it built up steadily as the Saturday approached and day by day we saw more and more Scots fans appearing, even though we were well north of London.

To learn I was in the team was another of the high points of my life.

Actually, we played the numbers game again. There was no change from the original choice against Ireland, but, for the third game in succession, I had a different number. This time it was No 6 and the line-up was: England – Clemence; Neal, Mills, Thompson, Watson, Wilkins, Keegan, Coppell, Latchford, Brooking, Barnes.

Scotland – Wood; Burley, F. Gray, Wark, McQueen, Hegarty, Dalglish, Souness, Jordan, Hartford, Graham.

Right away, I'll get the bad memory out of the way. We lost 3-1 with John Wark scoring for us and Barnes, Coppell and Keegan for them.

The Scotland fans were there in such numbers it was like a home from home; they gave us tremendous support, but by the end they were disgusted with us. On the day England were the better team without a doubt and I can assure any Scottish supporter who was there that they felt no worse than we did as we trooped off the park.

Barnes nicked his goal through a ruck of players just before half-time. I believe if we had gone in one up, as it looked after Wark's goal, we might well have won, but the 'lift' that goal gave England had to be seen to be believed.

That man Keegan took over second half. He was a different class and, as I found because I was marking him some of the time, he was the perfect example of perpetual motion. If he wasn't running at you he was trying to drag you out of position or heading for space shouting for the ball.

My direct opponent most of the time, though, was an old adversary, Bob Latchford, brother of Peter Latchford, the goalkeeper who was to give so many years of good service to Celtic.

Bob was the first striker I faced when I became a centre-half with Dundee United. This was in a friendly at Goodison arranged when Everton and United had a blank day after both being knocked out of our national Cup competitions.

He proved a big, strong, willing attacker that day and in this one at Wembley. He looked a bit lazy, but if you relaxed he would be past you in a flash.

I enjoyed both jousts with him and, as he didn't score, will quietly put it down to a points win for me!

Keegan did score and Coppell underlined England's superiority at Wembley, though. Steve Coppell is another of the little blokes I admire so much. He was totally unselfish, the complete team man playing wide on the right and doing everything so simply it looked easy. What a tragedy that he had to retire early because of knee trouble. That was a big blow to both Manchester United and England because there aren't many as good as him about.

My Wembley experience was bad in the scoreline sense, but it is a magic feeling to be out there. It had rained and the pitch was, as I had been warned, heavy. But I didn't notice, I was so proud to be playing for my country in a fixture that is extra-special.

And when I think over the number of times people say Wembley saps your strength, I don't think that is a physical thing, I believe it is down to the tension of appearing there.

No matter what game it is on that pitch, it is a highlight of a player's career – a Cup final, an international or whatever. If this gets to you, then you are tense and more easily tired out.

Personally, I'd be happy to play there any time!

15

Sickener in Norway

With a home international series which ended in Scotland having won one game and lost two, with a goal difference of two for, three against, my international career hadn't been exactly earth-shattering to date.

And things certainly didn't get very much better in the next couple of games – in fact in the second I hit one of the lowest points in my career so far.

I detail the game against Argentina elsewhere and my first experience of the little genius called Maradona. That game was at Hampden a week after the Wembley fixture.

Five days after that we were in action again – this time in my first international abroad. I knew what it was to travel in Europe with my club, now I was enjoying the experience with my country. Well, I was enjoying it up until I actually played!

The Norwegian people were friendly, the preparations for the game went well and the manager re-shaped the team. It was – Rough; Burley, Munro, Burns, McQueen, Gemmill, Graham, Dalglish, Jordan, Hartford, Robertson.

Archie Gemmill, another of the perpetual motion men, was back and it was one of John Robertson's early games for Scotland. Kenny Burns was alongside Gordon McQueen in mid-defence.

On the bench alongside me was John Wark.

With John Robertson in the kind of form that was a delight to watch, teasing defenders, nipping past them and sending over perfect crosses and with the quality of the opposition less than Argentina or England at Wembley it was no surprise that it was one of Scotland's more emphatic victories, 4-0 with the goals coming from Jordan, Dalglish, Robertson and McQueen.

Things were shaping well when we went into the dressing room at half-time.

What I didn't know was that George Burley was feeling ill. After he had been checked over by the doctor, manager Stein came to me and said, 'I know you haven't played there before, but how's about having a go at right back?'

He was right, I hadn't played there before, but said 'O.K.'

It was good to get out on to the pitch and be directly involved, but this must surely be one of the shortest international appearances on record.

Archie Gemmill knocked the ball through the Norwegian defence and I went on an overlap. It was my first positive move of the game.

I got to the ball all right, but when all my weight was on one leg Norwegian defender Aas, who was later to have a brief spell in English football, smashed into me with a tackle.

Even though I had been happily free of serious injury in my career to that point, I knew this was serious even when I was on the way down.

The pain was excruciating and trainer Donnie McKinnon barely looked before waving to the manager that I would have to go off.

So John Wark became the sub for the sub as I was carried to the dressing room. Doctor Fitzsimmons made a careful inspection in the dressing room, but it was too early to diagnose the exact trouble, even though I knew by the continuing pain that it wasn't something that would just go away.

We flew back to Glasgow that same night and I had the loneliest spot on any plane – a row of seats to myself with the injured leg propped up.

I had plenty of time to assess the tackle that caused the damage and it certainly didn't seem a fair one to me – not that this altered things much as far as the injury was concerned.

When we got to Glasgow, Donnie McKinnon took me straight to hospital where they put on a strong bandage.

As I was due to go on holiday to the south of France the very next day I was in a bit of a quandary, but a quick telephone call to manager Jim McLean and a return call a short time later o.k.'d my going on holiday with the order to 'watch yourself.'

Much though I enjoyed the break, the pain was still niggling away.

When I returned I went almost straight back into pre-season training. Things had seemed to be getting better, but the truth emerged when I broke down during a training session.

The trouble was diagnosed as a damaged medial cartilage in the left knee and it was removed in an operation in Bridge of Earn Hospital.

I wasn't long in hospital, five days to be exact, then it was back into light training and a gradual step up to full training. At the end of six weeks I thought I was right again . . . but I was kidding myself on.

I had lost a vital half-yard of pace and hard though I tried I just couldn't get it back.

It took a further six weeks before I really was ready and I realised I had made it in a practice game when I went into a hard tackle without thinking and came out the other side with the ball and no discomfort.

Naturally enough, with international matches to be played, manager Stein had to look elsewhere for people to play in my position.

First opponents in season 1979-80 were Peru at Hampden and the Scotland line-up was Rough; Jardine, Munro, Souness, McQueen, Burns, Cooper, Aitken, Dalglish, Hartford, Robertson (sub, Wark for Cooper). It was a 1-1 draw with Olaechea scoring an own goal for Scotland.

Next it was Austria, again at Hampden, and again a 1-1 draw with Archie Gemmill scoring. The team this time was – Rough; Jardine, Munro, Souness, McQueen, Burns, Wark, Gemmill, Dalglish, Graham, Robertson. Sub was Cooper for Graham.

In November, 1979, Belgium were hosts to Scotland and we lost 2-0. The team was Rough; Jardine, Munro, Wark, Hansen, Miller, Dalglish, Souness, Jordan, Hartford, Robertson, with Frank Gray and Provan going on for Munro and Jordan.

The Belgians returned to Hampden a month later and though John Robertson got a goal, the result was a 3-1 defeat. This time, the team was Rough, Jardine, McGrain, Wark, McQueen, Burns, Dalglish, Aitken, Derek Johnstone, Bannon, Robertson. Provan went on for Bannon as substitute.

An excellent victory followed in March, 1980 – 4-1 over Portugal at Hampden, with Dalglish, Gray, Archibald, Gemmill getting the goals. This time the team was – Rough; Burley, McGrain, Narey, McLeish, Hansen, Dalglish, Souness, Andy Gray, Gemmill, Robertson. Archibald and Provan took the places of Dalglish and Robertson during the game.

Then it was into the home international series and a bad start with a 1-0 defeat from Northern Ireland in Belfast. The Scotland team – Thomson, Burley, McGrain, Narey, McLeish, Souness, Strachan, Archibald, Dalglish, Gemmill, Weir – subs Jordan and Provan for Souness and Weir.

All season I had been working away at my game, settling back down after the injury – and keeping a close watch on the international scene.

And, suddenly, I was back in – against Wales at Hampden. It was May 21, almost exactly 50 weeks since I had been carried off in Norway, and the team was – Rough, McGrain, Munro, Hegarty, Miller, McLeish, Strachan, Gemmill, Dalglish, Jordan, Weir – sub Aitken for Weir.

Playing alongside Alex McLeish and Willie Miller was a great experience in itself. Often I have heard arguments over whether they, at the centre of Aberdeen's defence for so long, are better than Dave Narey and myself, who have been in the same position for Dundee United over many seasons.

It isn't for me to judge. Looking at them I can recall few mistakes they have made, very few. There is a difference in character between the two pairings, too. They are more outgoing and outspoken, we are quieter and probably less noticeable.

The arguments will go on and on as to which is the better central defence. What I will say is they are good – and we aren't at all bad either.

But back to the first time we played together . . .

It was a good result, a 1-0 win. The Welsh team was Davies, Nicholas, J. Jones, Yorath, Pontin, Price, Giles, Flynn, Walsh, James, M. Thomas.

There was no John Toshack this time. I wish there had been because I feel we would have coped better than we did a year earlier at Cardiff.

There was, however, a substitution. Striker Walsh went off and a young lad not many of us had heard of took his place. I can't honestly say I appreciated just how talented he was – it was his first cap – but I do recall he was sharp and stretched us several times when the ball came through to him.

His name – Ian Rush. From that point his career rocketed until he moved to Juventus after a wonderful spell with Liverpool.

In a way that was an eventful debut, but even more eventful was the Scotland goal.

I'll take a separate paragraph to state – IT WAS SCORED BY WILLIE MILLER.

Willie must have got nosebleed getting himself so far up the park, but he did score. The details? I can't remember, I was so surprised at the event!

Seriously, though, I feel if he had made more runs like he did here during his career he would have netted a fair number of goals. He has, when the situation is right, a great ability to get into danger areas in the opposing last third of the field.

I didn't know it at the time, but my international career at full cap level was nearly over.

There was only one other game to come that season and one against Northern Ireland in a sudden 'one-off' recall in 1983.

We were determined to avenge the 3-1 defeat at Wembley a year earlier and, on paper, our chances looked good.

The line-ups were: Scotland – Rough; McGrain, Munro, Hegarty, McLeish, Miller, Strachan, Aitken, Dalglish, Jordan, Gemmill.

England – Clemence; Cherry, Sansom, Thomson, Watson, Wilkins, Coppell, McDermott, Johnson, Mariner, Brooking.

Burley for Munro and Andy Gray for Aitken were our subs, Hughes for Mariner theirs.

There was no Keegan to harry the life out of us this time, but there was a bloke with exactly the opposite approach – Trevor Brooking. He moved like a strolling city gent, but his control of the ball and his ability to send away effective passes was something else.

It was his turn this time to take star rating – and score a goal. The result was a 2-0 defeat with Steve Coppell getting their other counter.

In my final 'big' international against Northern Ireland in Glasgow in May, 1983, I did team up with Dave Narey for once and we played in front of the man who is in goal for Dundee United now, Billy Thomson. I also achieved a new peak of being made captain, certainly as great a personal 'high' as any in my career.

The line-up was – Thomson; Dawson, Gough, Simpson, Hegarty, Narey, Wark, Bannon, Andy Gray, Burns, Nicholas. The result was a 0-0 draw, but the fact that four Dundee United players were in the team – Gough, Narey, Bannon and myself – proved the increasing notice that was being taken of our performances as a club.

And if you add the fact that Andy Gray had been a United player and Billy Thomson was to become one, it was quite an occasion.

My only surprise now is that, as a United player, Thomson hasn't yet started to be capped again. I know there are several good 'keepers around, but there are none better.

I had a brief return to the international arena last season with outings as an over-age player for the Under 21's against West Germany at Ibrox and Belgium in Bruges.

For that honour I thank Andy Roxburgh, the current Scotland boss, and Craig Brown, his assistant. It really was a pleasure to work alongside Craig and Tommy Craig on the coaching side of things and to play alongside such emerging talents as our own Kevin

Gallacher, Robert Fleck, Derek Ferguson, Derek Whyte and Chelsea's Gordon Durie. They, among others, give me a lot of hope for the future.

Finally, what of Jock Stein, the man who guided Scotland's fortunes for so long and who was to die so tragically in a moment of triumph in Wales?

He was a man with a presence. You could sense that he had been successful even though he never talked about it. There was a sort of air about him. I see the same in the man who captained his most successful Celtic team, Billy McNeill, now back at Parkhead as Boss.

Jock was in a different class at handling experienced big-name players. He gave them respect, he gave everyone respect, but he was the man in charge and it was extremely unwise even to doubt it.

He had his own way of doing things, but he would never talk down to any player while at the same time cracking down hard if anyone stepped out of line.

We had one player, who had over 30 caps by the time he finished, who was very fussy over such things as the rooms he occupied. I can't remember any bad ones, but he was quick to mention it if he thought things weren't just right.

The manager respected his viewpoint, but, in the end, it was always he, not the player, who allocated the accommodation. And his word was final.

A man I am privileged to have worked with and for, and a great loss to the game.

16

The Honours . . . So Far!

The honours list of any provincial club will never compare with those from the big cities, but I believe that our honours list tells those same big city clubs that they can never take anything for granted.

We won the league title in season 1982-83 and the League Cup in 1979-80 and 1980-81 – and we have been there or thereabout in both those competitions and the Scottish Cup on many other occasions.

Without doubt the highlight of my club career so far was the winning of the Premier League championship.

That is the real mark of a club's ability. To play throughout a season in all sorts of weather on all sorts of pitches, home and away, and emerge at the end with most points.

And not only did we do it that season, but I played in all 36 league games, which gives me an extra boost at a personal level.

The icing on this particular cake was that the actual game in which we won it was at Dens Park against our local rivals Dundee. I'll never forget that day.

I was up around 9.30 which is my usual time when we have a game in Dundee, for my cereal, tea and toast breakfast along with a look at the newspapers.

They were full of speculation about our chances as Rangers, Celtic and Aberdeen were all close enough to us to ruin everything (for us, that is) if we lost. I think the United fans were frightened to speculate . . . after all if we did it, it was the first time in the club's history that the league title had come to Tannadice and they had experience of there being many a slip . . .

After a tea and toast lunch-time snack and good wishes from the family, I drove off to a car park near Tannadice with more good wishes coming from several people who recognised me as I was driving along.

As usual we made our way to Dens by walking up the road, and again came the good wishes, and some other opinions expressed by people sporting Dundee's colours!

Celtic and Rangers are used to winning titles, we were new to the game, so there was no pattern for us to follow other than to keep the thought of one game at a time in our mind and prepare for it as we always did.

The manager certainly followed that route. He never over-stresses the importance of any game and didn't this time, giving his usual comments on general play and a few individual points.

As a pre-match ritual I like a rub down from our physio, at the time Andy Dickson. It always makes me feel more relaxed. I had that and began to get ready.

I probably was more tense than usual, but wouldn't admit it to myself, though I clearly remember being in full strip more quickly than usual.

At seven minutes to three we were ready to go out, with me as captain leading. And as we started trotting down the ramp leading from the dressing room area to the running track, then the pitch at Dens, the noise hit us like a physical blow.

I love playing there and this time it was a 29,000 crowd, every one of them, it seemed, roaring at the top of his voice. It was a marvellous feeling to be at the centre of that kind of emotion.

I was feeling good, realising that I was at the stage so many players dream about and hope to achieve – to be a playing member of a team with one game between them and the championship of their country.

I had seen no signs of nerves in the dressing room or in the kick-about, yet we started nervously, which proves you never know reaction until games actually start.

Fortunately that didn't last long. After about 15 minutes we picked up the rhythm all good teams show and I felt it was only a matter of time before we scored.

When we did, it was real Roy of the Rovers stuff by the man who snatched so many vital goals for us by improvising something on the spur of the moment, Ralph Milne.

He got the ball in our half, moved forward, saw keeper Colin Kelly had come off his line and, cool as a cucumber, chipped the ball high over his head and into the net.

Our second goal came from the penalty spot. Kelly saved Eamonn Bannon's shot, but Eammon was on to the rebound like a flash and netted.

Second half we stuck the ball about, making it difficult for them, making them chase ... and got a real fright when they scored through Ferguson.

As the minutes ticked away, I could see the Boss and Wattie Smith jumping about in the dug-out, playing every single ball, willing us on. We couldn't hear them, but knew what they were saying!!!

Dundee came more and more into the game and I kept taking the odd glance at the clock at the Tannadice end of the ground. I'll swear the hands never moved for the last 15 mintues – until they suddenly jumped forward and I heard three blasts of the referee's whistle.

Suddenly, all hell broke loose. First there was Hamish McAlpine, Dave Narey and me, then other players, the manager, Wattie, fans, fans and more fans. I wish to this day they hadn't been quite so quick to fill the pitch. We wanted to do a lap of honour, but it was impossible. I appreciate their feelings on a day like that, but a lap to every corner of the ground where your supporters are gives everyone the chance to see the trophy and the players who won it for them.

As I accepted the league championship trophy and held it high in the air to an explosion of sound, I had a quiet moment of thought to myself that all the hard work, all the training, all the effort had really been worth it.

That night we were due to appear at a dance in Alyth and most players went there and afterwards to Frank Kopel's house for a party.

There were a few 'sair heids' in the morning, but we actually played in a testimonial game at Forfar the next day. It had been arranged long before we knew we were to win the title.

And what happened? We got a right old verbal hammering from the Boss who reckoned that, though we won, we hadn't played well. He excepted Richard Gough.

It seemed a bit rough to us, but that's the way he is.

Our first major honour was the League Cup win three years before the league title, in season 1979-80. We first played a 0-0 draw with Aberdeen at Hampden in a game which they deserved to win, but which didn't exactly come into the category of memorable.

When it was agreed that the replay would be at Dens, no one realised this was to be our happy hunting ground then and in the future, with two League Cup and one title win achieved on our 'away' pitch in the city of Dundee.

To be perfectly honest the replay was a bit of a let down. We have had many great games against Aberdeen over recent years, but this was one of our easiest victories.

The result was 3-0, our scorers Pettigrew (2) and Sturrock, but where Aberdeen's form went that night, I'll never know.

In fairness, we hit a peak with Paul Sturrock, ably assisted by Willie Pettigrew up front, taking the Dons defence apart.

When Paul is in the form he was in that night he is almost unstoppable. The pitch was heavy, the way we like it and the way he likes it. He jinked, and twisted and turned, and laid off the ball in a display that, had it been by a Brazilian, would have earned inches deep headlines in the world Press.

It was a great moment for me personally to go up as team captain and be presented with the first major trophy the club had won in its entire history.

Another important aspect of winning the League Cup is that it guarantees entry into Europe with around two-thirds of the season still to go and your targets narrowed down to winning the Scottish Cup or the league.

To gain entry into the following season's European competitions via the league or the Cup you might have to wait until the very last day of the season.

The major competition might be the European Champions Cup, which means winning the league title, but it is nice to know that you are in the UEFA Cup tournament as early as ten months before you are due to play your first game.

A year later we were back at Dens Park in the final of the 1980-81 League Cup with our opponents this time our local rivals Dundee.

I have been asked since it we didn't feel it a bit unfair that we had to go out and try to win on our opponents' pitch, that we had, in effect, to play away while they were at home in a Cup final, normally played on a neutral ground.

My answer is always 'no', because we like Dens Park and never feel it is an away ground. It is only a walk up the road from Tannadice and we can follow the same pre-match routine as if we were playing at home.

There is a slope, it is different to Tannadice in many ways, but we know the pitch and its surrounds ... and we certainly have a great record there, which proves my point.

Whatever, on that second League Cup final occasion both Dundee and ourselves fancied our chances very strongly. Us because we had won the trophy the year before, them because Donald Mackay, a former United 'keeper now in charge of Blackburn Rovers, seemed to have built a good squad of players and there was promise of better days to come after a lean spell.

Of course, if you don't fancy yourselves you shouldn't be in finals!

Again, though, it was our night. Another 3-0 victory on a wintry, frozen ground this time.

My contribution was more positive this time, too – a direct assist in two of the goals. The first came when Graeme Payne took a corner, I got my head to the ball and it dropped down off the crossbar for Paul Sturrock to tuck away.

The second was similar. The ball came over, I got a flick to it and it went to Paul again, who again stuck it in the net. Our other scorer was Davie Dodds.

It was a freezing cold day, snow had been threatening all day, but that win warmed us up perfectly.

I didn't, even though I was still club captain, accept the trophy this time, though.

Earlier in the week we had a players' meeting at which our longest-serving player, goalkeeper Hamish McAlpine, was deliberately not present. That was because at the meeting we decided that, should we win the Cup, he would get the honour of going up to collect it.

As we trooped up for the presentation, the rest of us suddenly stopped. 'Come on then', said Hamish. 'No . . . you go on', he was told.

When he realised what was happening he didn't seem to know what to do. Then he was off and when the fans spotted who was getting the Cup, the roar almost lifted the roof off the Dens stand. To say Hamish was pretty chuffed as well is putting it mildly.

One other personal point about this final. By the time it was played, video recordings of matches were the 'in' thing. There hadn't been one of the game the year before, but there was one of this final.

I contacted a friend who got a copy for me and, occasionally, I play it over. No, not as an ego trip, but to show Paul, Mark and Christopher how young their Dad looked in his prime!

The teams and scorers in the three games in which we won our three trophies were:

League title – Dundee United – McAlpine; Stark, Malpas, Gough, Hegarty, Narey, Bannon, Milne, Kirkwood, Sturrock (Holt), Dodds. Scorers – Milne, Bannon (pen).

Dundee – Kelly; Glennie (Mackie), McKimmie, Fraser, Smith, Macdonald, Ferguson, McGeachie, Sinclair, Kidd, Stephen. Scorer – Ferguson.

First League Cup – Dundee United – McAlpine; Stark, Kopel, Phillip (Fleming), Hegarty, Narey, Bannon, Sturrock, Pettigrew, Holt, Payne (Murray).

Aberdeen – Clark; Kennedy, Rougvie, McLeish, Gardner, Miller, Strachan, Archibald, McGhee (Jarvie), McMaster (Hamilton), Scanlon.

Replay – United – McAlpine; Stark, Kopel, Fleming, Hegarty, Narey, Bannon, Sturrock, Pettigrew, Holt, Payne (Kirkwood). Scorers – Pettigrew 2, Sturrock.

Aberdeen – Clark; Kennedy, Rougvie, McLeish, Gardner, Miller, Strachan, Archibald, McGhee (Jarvie), McMaster, Scanlon (Hamilton).

Second League Cup – Dundee United – McAlpine; Holt, Kopel, Phillip, Hegarty, Narey, Bannon, Payne, Pettigrew, Sturrock, Dodds. Scorers – Dodds, Sturrock (2).

Dundee – Geddes; Barr, Schaedler, Fraser, Glennie, McGeachie, Mackie, Stephen, Sinclair, Williamson (Shirra), A. Geddes (Scrimgeour).

17

. . . *and Finally*

As you will have seen from my story so far, football has been, overall, great to me – and I, in turn, have tried to give the game my maximum in effort and ability.

I have played with and against hundreds, maybe even thousands of players in my time and the amazing fact is that only the merest handful have come into the category of people I don't like.

In fact, only one, who must remain nameless, hits the ten out of ten category in being unpopular with me.

He is the player, now out of the playing side of the game, who turned and deliberately spat in my face during a match.

In the heat of the moment, things happen out on the field that you'd rather didn't, but this bloke did what he did coldly and calmly. Of all the low-life things, spitting at an opponent, to me, is it.

It is a simple fact that there is more of my career as a player behind me than in front, but that does not mean in any way that I am contemplating the end of my playing days.

I believe you must be enthusiastic even on the dullest training day and I am still that, I still find training enjoyable.

When you are looking ahead, you must discount injury and illness, of course. They can, as so sadly happens in the case of players like my former club colleague Derek Stark and, more recently, Davie Provan of Celtic, bring things to a sudden stop.

Allowing for that, I would like to play for as long as, say, Sandy Jardine, who is four years older than me and still doing an excellent job for Hearts.

I believe that, whereas in the old days a player was rated 'over the hill' as soon as he hit 30, the playing age in many cases is now deep into your 30s . . . in the case of goalkeepers it hit 40 with Pat Jennings and looks like doing it again with Peter Shilton.

But my playing days will come to an end – regretfully – some time.

And that is when I would like to get involved in the other side of the game in some capacity . . . coaching, maybe even managing.

I appreciate how difficult it is to be successful in that side of the game, but I would most certainly like to give it a try.

Meantime, though, it is on with the game and, hopefully, the collecting of a few more club honours to put in the memory bank.

Paul's Playing Record

His career began with Hamilton some 15 years ago as a striker and his success in that role led United to persuade him to give up his career in insurance and try full-time football. It was a step that looked a gamble until a friendly match at Goodison in November, 1976, changed his fortunes. Paul stepped back to central defence with great success and that has brought Paul International honours as well as the distinction of being the only Tannadice captain to lift a major trophy, captaining the club to all three honours to date.

FACT FILE:

Born: 25/7/1954.
Place of Birth: Edinburgh.
Height: 5′10½″.
Weight: 10st. 12lbs.
Previous Clubs: Tynecastle Boys' Club, Hamilton Accies.
Date Signed: 12/11/74 for a £40,000 fee.
Debut for Club: League: 16/11/74 as sub. v. Partick Thistle (A).

Premier: 13/9/75 as sub. v. Aberdeen (A). Scottish Cup: 24/1/76 v. Hamilton (H). League Cup 13/8/75 as sub. v. Partick Thistle (A).

European Cup: 14/9/83 v. Hamrun Spartans (A). U.E.F.A. Cup: 23/9/75 v. Keflavik (A).

First Goal: League 7/12/74 v. Clyde (H) in 3-3 draw. Premier: On his debut at Pittodrie.

Scottish Cup: On his debut at home to Hamilton. League Cup: 21/8/76 v. Dumbarton in 2-1 win.

U.E.F.A. Cup: 30/9/75 v. Keflavik (H) in 4-0 win. U.E.F.A. Cup Runners-up Medal (1986-87).

Honours: Premier Division Champions, 1982/83. League Cup: Winners 1979/80 and 1980/81; Runners-up 1981/82 and 1984/85. Scottish Cup: Runners-up 1980/81, 1984/85 and 1986/87.

International Caps: Eight full – 1979 v. Wales, N. Ireland, England, Argentina, Norway (sub.); 1980 v. Wales, England; 1983, N. Ireland. League Cup – 1980 v. Irish League.
Scotland's Players' Player of the Year, 1979.

Appearance Record:

		League		*Scottish Cup*		*League Cup*		*European Cup*		*U.E.F.A. Cup*		*Anglo Scottish*		*Total*	
		Aps	*Gls*	*Aps*	*Gls*	*Aps*	*Gls*	*Aps*	*Gls*	*Aps*	*Gls*	*Aps*	*Gls*	*Aps*	*Gls*
Hamilton	1972/73	36	7	4	1	4	—	—	—	—	—	—	—	44	8
Hamilton	1973/74	31	10	2	—	4	—	—	—	—	—	—	—	37	10
Hamilton	1974/75	12	5	—	—	6	7	—	—	—	—	—	—	18	12
United	1974/75	10(7)	4	1(1)	—	—	—	—	—	—	—	—	—	11(8)	4
United	1975/76	31(2)	8	3	1	3	—	—	—	3	2	—	—	40(2)	11
United	1976/77	36	6	1	—	6	3	—	—	—	—	2	—	45	9
United	1977/78	36	4	4	2	8	3	—	—	2	—	—	—	50	9
United	1978/79	36	5	1	—	2	—	—	—	2	—	—	—	41	5
United	1979/80	27	—	2	—	7	2	—	—	4	—	—	—	40	2
United	1980/81	33	3	7	2	11	4	—	—	4	1	—	—	55	10
United	1981/82	36	2	5	—	6(1)	—	—	—	8	2	—	—	55(1)	4
United	1982/83	36	3	1	—	10	—	—	—	8	2	—	—	55	5
United	1983/84	36	4	3	—	10	—	8	—	—	—	—	—	57	4
United	1984/85	33	2	5	—	6	—	—	—	6	3	—	—	50	5
United	1985/86	36	5	5	—	5	—	—	—	6	1	—	—	52	6
United	1986/87	21(2)	4	3	1	4	—	—	—	6(1)	—	—	—	34(3)	5

Dundee United's European Record

EUROPEAN CUP

The Premier Trophy and we will remember our only entry so far as it saw us reach the furthest stage from any of our 15 years of entry in European competition. Our home record as you can see was unblemished.

SUMMARY

	P	W	D	L	F	A
Home	4	4	0	0	10	0
Away	4	1	1	2	4	5
	8	5	1	2	14	5

14/9/83 Hamrun Spartans.

McAlpine, Kirkwood, Stark 1, Gough, Hegarty, Narey, Bannon 1, Milne, Reilly 1, Holt, Dodds, (Clark, Taylor)

Result 3-0 (Stark, Bannon, Reilly).

28/9/83 Hamrun Spartans.

McAlpine, Kirkwood 1, Murray, Gough, Hegarty, Stark, Bannon, Milne 2, Holt, Sturrock, Dodds, (Payne).

Result 3-0 (Kirkwood, Milne).

19/10/83 Standard Liege.

McAlpine, Kirkwood, Stark, Gough, Hegarty, Narey, Bannon, Milne, Malpas, Holt, Dodds.

2/11/83 Standard Liege.

McAlpine, Kirkwood, Stark, Gough, Hegarty 1, Narey, Bannon, Milne 2, Malpas, Holt, Dodds 1, (Reilly).

Result 4-0 (Hegarty, Milne, Dodds).

7/3/84 SK Rapid.

McAlpine, Stark 1, Malpas, Gough, Hegarty, Narey, Bannon, Milne, Kirkwood, Sturrock, Dodds, (Holt, Clark).

Result 1-2 (Stark).

21/3/84 SK Rapid.

McAlpine, Stark, Malpas, Gough, Hegarty, Narey, Bannon, Kirkwood, Coyne, Sturrock, Dodds 1, (Holt, Milne).

Result 1-0 (Dodds).

11/4/84 A.S. Roma.
McAlpine, Stark 1, Malpas, Gough, Hegarty, Narey, Bannon, Milne, Kirkwood, Sturrock, Dodds 1, (Coyne)
Result 2-0 (Stark, Dodds).
25/4/84 A.S. Roma.
McAlpine, Stark, Malpas, Gough, Hegarty, Narey, Bannon, Milne, Kirkwood, Sturrock, Dodds, (Holt, Clark).
Result 0-3.

EUROPEAN CUP WINNERS CUP

Although the Scottish Cup is the one major honour to have eluded us, we have made one appearance in this European tourney. A 3-0 defeat by Celtic in the 1974 Scottish Cup Final did have the consolation of automatic entry to Europe, as Celtic had completed the League and Cup double. The tie with Juil Petrosani was the first under the emergent talent within the Club as youngsters Dave Narey, Andy Gray and Paul Sturrock got their taste of the European scene.

SUMMARY

	P	W	D	L	F	A
Home	2	1	1	0	3	0
Away	2	0	0	2	0	3
	4	1	1	2	3	3

18/9/74 Juil Petrosani.
McAlpine, Rolland, Kopel, Copland 1, Smith, Narey 1, Houston, Gardner 1, Gray, Fleming, McDonald, (Sturrock, McLeod).
Result 3-0 (Copland, Narey, Gardner).
2/10/74 Juil Petrosani.
McAlpine, Rolland, Kopel, Copland, Smith, Narey, Knox, Gardner, Gray, Fleming, McDonald, (Traynor).
Result 0-2.
23/10/74 Borsapor.
McAlpine, Rolland, Kopel, Copland, Smith, Houston, Traynor, Narey, Gray, Knox, McDonald, (Payne).
Result 0-0.
6/11/74 Borsapor.
McAlpine, Rolland, Kopel, Copland, Smith, Houston, Payne, W. Smith, Gray, Fleming, Traynor, (Narey, McDonald).
Result 0-1.

FAIRS CITIES/UEFA CUP

The trophy in which we have been such regular entrants over the past 21 years. We have now overtaken Hibs to become the most experienced side in this competition, with 13 entries to the competition many rightly regard as the hardest to win.

Index